The Meatless Galley Cookbook

The Meatless Galley Cookbook

by

Anne Carlson

Seaworthy Publications

Brookfield, Wisconsin

Illustrations by Bob Stewart

Published in the USA by:

Seaworthy Publications
17125C W. Bluemound Rd.
Suite 200
Brookfield, WI. 53008-0949

The publisher wishes to express thanks to John Lanier, a close friend of the author, who wrote the Foreword and furnished the Title Page illustration of "Sandpiper" at anchor.

All other illustrations including the cover painting are licensed for use in this book by Bob Stewart, marine artist and owner of Waterfront Gallery, 116 E. Grand Ave., Port Washington, Wisconsin, 53074.

Library of Congress Cataloging-in-Publication Data

Carlson, Anne, 1930-
  The meatless galley cookbook / by Anne Carlson.
    p.   cm.
  Includes   index.
  ISBN 0-9639566-2-0
  1. Cookery, Marine. 2. Vegetarianism. I. Title.
TX840.M7C34   1995
  641.5'753—dc20

                                                    95-30807
                                                      CIP

To your dreams--
and to the memories
of the dreams
you dared to dream...

Foreword

Twenty years ago a friend telephoned to say—rather urgently—that there was a woman with a sailboat down at the yacht club who was looking for a navigator to sail with her to Hawaii. Twenty-four hours later I was on the high seas with Anne Carlson, helping to deliver a 27-foot cutter a couple of thousand miles to Maui. My main concern wasn't the diminutive size of our vessel, nor my new shipmate's sailing ability, but rather, *how on earth are we going to eat?* The sea was rough, there was no standing headroom below, no gimballed stove, not even a table to eat on. Just finding a can opener seemed to call for heroic measures. But Anne gamely served up a hot meal in those primitive conditions, the first of many thousands I have had the pleasure of sharing with her.

My previous sailing adventures had featured cuisine similar to that found in London during the Blitz, and in my ignorance I had assumed that this was just the way things are when you go horizon-chasing. Sling aboard a sack of potatoes, some onions and beans and a case of corned beef, and you're off to Patagonia (or wherever). But Anne refuses to live that way on her own boat, the "Sandpiper." To my astonishment, we ate on real ceramic plates, with placemats and cloth napkins. My mind reeled at the sight of spice bottles employed on a daily basis. Eating aboard a small boat didn't have to be a purely utilitarian exercise after all.

Unfortunately, I was all too content to simply enjoy the food as we slowly cruised our way around the world, and I didn't pay particularly close attention to how Anne painstakingly planned the meals, assembled the ingredients, and then actually *cooked* the darned stuff. Later, when I found myself as a bachelor back in the "real world," my goose was cooked. Anne very generously started mailing me recipes to help stave off malnutrition, and thus a cookbook was born.

If you're a young male, this book could be a real lifesaver. In fact, its appeal should be universal. Ideally, you are about to set sail for Tahiti with your sweetie, and it's just occured to you that there are very few restaurants along the way. But you could just as well be setting out for Alaska in a camper, or dragging a trailer down to Baja. This is good, hearty, wholesome fare, and you don't need microprocessor-controlled equipment to prepare it. Enjoy, and keep a close eye on the waterfront . . .

John Lanier
Port of Spain, Trinidad
May, 1995

CONTENTS

Introduction

Introduction

In a distant port, a fellow yachtie once said to me, "I feel like I am eating my way around the world." Food is a major topic of conversation with people everywhere, but it is especially so with yachtsmen. On arrival in a new harbor, the first question from the kids: "Where is the nearest snack bar?" The Captain wants to know: "Where's the best restaurant?" The ship's cook asks: "Where is the market? How are the prices?" and "Do they deliver?"

On a boat, food and all of its aspects take up a considerable amount of one's time. Meal planning, shopping, transporting food from market to your boat, stowing, cooking, and finally cleaning up (and *properly* disposing of the garbage) are all links in the boater's "food chain."

Food involves more than just eating! Whether of major or minor importance to you, casual or formal, we all have to have it. And someone aboard has to be responsible for it. On a small boat it can be a challenge to stow, prepare, and serve it.

How to provision a boat for a passage or a casual cruise is a very personal matter involving both practical considerations and individual food preferences. However, from my own experiences, I can offer you some useful thoughts on managing a galley on a small boat.

My first boat was a 21-foot trailer-sailer in which I enjoyed many short weekend cruises around Lake Tahoe, California, and a three-week venture to Baja California, Mexico. I began my provisioning education with that trip, learning which foods kept well, which were easiest to prepare, and which items weren't worth taking along. I moved aboard my current boat, "Sandpiper," in 1973. She is 29-feet long, and I have made several passages of 2700 miles or more in her. My longest passage was 35 days, crossing through the doldrums from Cabo San Lucas, Baja California, to French Polynesia; another was 26 days from Lanzarote in the Canary Islands, across the Atlantic to Martinique, West Indies. There were many 10-day or shorter passages in the South Pacific, such as from

Bora Bora to Samoa, from Fiji to Vanuatu, and across the Coral Sea from the Solomon Islands to Australia.

I have never had a shortage of food while in passage, and we always ate very well. Our diets were healthful, and we never have had any illness aboard, including fatigue, body sores, colds, or "flu." I attribute this to a healthful diet and good personal hygiene. The only time we experienced sore throats was after a long passage and we enjoyed that cold beer at the Yacht Club upon arrival at our first port. I eventually learned to drink from the can or bottle until my body had time to adjust to the new environment and its different microbes.

We do take multivitamins, but we also eat properly. There are many foods that, with a little care, keep quite well. But on a small boat with limited space you need to be selective. You can't afford to carry food you know you might have to throw out, or food that keeps well but nobody likes to eat.

Whether you are embarking on a lengthy passage or a leisurely weekend cruise, I hope some of the following information will be of interest to you. Even if you plan to eat most of your meals in restaurants, you should have *some* food on board if only for emergency use. With careful planning even a small boat can provide hearty meals.

Water

The first consideration in your provisions planning should be fresh water. Many people ask me how we managed to carry enough water on our 35-day crossing. We left with 60 gallons and arrived with 60 gallons! We didn't plan on that, so the first few days we were very careful with water. I had a salt water pump in my galley, and we even brushed our teeth with sea water as well as using it for washing dishes and some for cooking. We did, however, use a small amount of fresh water for a daily wipe down of our bodies—just a splash in a bowl to dampen a wash cloth. It was worth it.

Then we got into the ITCZ, the Intertropical Convergence Zone. It rained and rained, and when I saw the volume of water squirting out of the drain in the cockpit seat and then pouring directly into my sea boots, I called for a bucket. Thus began our collection of rain water. We never have been very organized about catching rain water at sea, finding that the torrential amount of rain from one giant cumulonimbus made complicated rain catchers unnecessary—we just put buckets in strategic places and soon wished we had more five-gallon jugs to fill! But given the importance of this fresh water bonanza, a bit of forethought would be worthwhile. Just remember that this sort of tropical downpour normally has a blast of wind associated with it, so don't count on using your sails as rain collectors. We stopped brushing our teeth with sea water and took refreshing rain baths instead of bowl baths, about the only positive aspect of spending 12 days becalmed in the doldrums.

But you can not depend on rain on every passage, so you do need to provide for enough water for your planned time en route, plus a bit extra for a safety margin. Remember, you probably will—or should—drink more water at sea than you usually do. For cooking, you can use the liquid from many canned foods to add to the cooking water for rice and pulses. Also, you can use a small amount of sea water for cooking pasta and rice. If you have a pressure cooker (which I think is an essential), you can use sea water for steaming potatoes and other vegetables.

There are many articles and studies done on how much water one needs for survival. As for relatively comfortable living, I feel one gallon per day is reasonable for two people. That gives plenty of water for drinking and cooking (in addition to some sea water and juices from canned foods) plus a little for a "bowl bath." You might not use that much every day; some days you might use more.

So, how much water should you have? On a small cruising boat the answer is simple: all you can carry! I fill my 28-gallon water tank, then carry several separate water Jerry jugs in the event the tank or one of the jugs breaks or becomes contaminated. I always double the amount of water I anticipate needing for a passage, just in case the trip takes longer than planned due to unfavorable weather or a dismasting. If you have planned well, you will have plenty of extra water to splurge on a marvelous fresh water bath when you finally drop anchor at the end of the passage.

Provisioning for the Passage

Planning for the Shopping Trip

Each of us has our preferences as to what we like to eat at sea. To provision for a passage or cruise, my suggestion is that you plan a seven day menu to include three meals a day, plus snacks and a night-watch meal. Then, make a list of all items and quantities you need for each meal for the number of persons you will be feeding. Repeat the menu as necessary for the number of days of your planned passage, remembering to plan for a few extra days for safety. Total the items, then make your shopping list accordingly. Separate your list into two parts: fresh food and packaged foods. Dried and packaged foods like rice, pulses, spices, tea, coffee, and canned goods can be bought and stowed ahead of time, but fresh foods should be bought as close to departure time as possible. Try to find eggs that have not been refrigerated or washed of their natural protective coating. Call the "farm" and asked them to put aside some eggs especially for you to fetch on your final shopping day. Equally important, look for a supply of vegetables that are fresh from the farm and have not been refrigerated. You'll be surprised how people will become interested in your provisioning project as well as your sailing plans, and will be more than willing to try to accommodate you.

I have a master shopping list that I use especially when shopping for a passage. I also find it handy for weekly shopping, when I use it for a checklist to help me recall those items I might have forgotten. It has evolved over the years, and I find it indispensable. My list has almost everything I need with the exception of a few exotic items that I might fancy, if I happen to see them.

Fresh Food

There are many vegetables and fruits that keep quite well on a long passage, and you should carry as many of these as stowage space allows. The quality of life improves markedly if you can prepare your meals with fresh foods. They do take up a lot of space, and there are times on a rough passage when it is much easier just to open a can, but you will find that you can use fresh food virtually every day. Just chopping a small bit of fresh carrot or onion into canned peas enhances the dish. Add a bit of basil, mint, or nutmeg and the crew will think you trained in Paris.

At sea I find a one-pot meal is not only easier to prepare, but also more comfortable to eat in a tossing boat. You can mix a selection of canned foods with fresh ones and have a superb meal. Many of the recipes in this book can be made using canned foods in place of some of the fresh ones: carrots, corn, green beans, potatoes, and peas are all easily substituted.

On my most recent passage, across the Atlantic, I provisioned heavily with fresh foods in the Canary Islands, and we arrived in Martinique with quite a bit left in the veggie basket. I did give attention to perishable items every day, throwing out anything that had spoiled and using immediately those that were obviously on their last day. I didn't have to reject much during the passage, but I was fortunate to have a source of very fresh, un-refrigerated victuals where I provisioned. I wrapped almost everything in newspaper, which I have found to be the best way to keep vegetables fresh. I stowed them in a large basket open to the air, or in a cool, well-ventilated place. Paper sacks are also good for storage. During my crossing to French Polynesia, I found that potatoes and onions stowed in plastic buckets began to rot. Plastic buckets don't have enough ventilation, allowing moisture to condense and run down the inside of the bucket. Similarly, I have not had good luck with vegetables shrink-wrapped in Styrofoam tubs. Suspending fresh vegetables in netting is a popular notion, but on my size boat not very practical.

Vegetables which I found to "hang in there" for a trans-oceanic passage are the following: potatoes, yams, onions, garlic, ginger, cabbages, squash, pumpkin, and beets. These should, with care, last 30 days or even longer. Eggs are also included in this category if they are very fresh, unwashed, and stored in a cool and well-ventilated part of the boat. Simply turn the egg cartons over every few days. I have never done anything more than that, and I have enjoyed good eggs four weeks after departure.

Vegetables which will last for about two to three weeks when properly stored are: Brussels sprouts, carrots, peppers, leeks, beets, tomatoes (buy them at various stages of ripeness), zucchini, and eggplant.

Celery, green onions, green beans, lettuce, and fresh peas last only a few days in the tropics; but of course if you are cruising in cooler areas you will find everything lasts longer (I spent a year in Denmark and found my vegetables froze if I left my veggie basket in the cockpit overnight. My refrigerator was the whole out-of-doors).

Fruits are always a pleasure on a passage, and many keep very well. Individually wrapped apples, oranges, limes, lemons, cantaloupe, avocado, grapefruit, and watermelon should keep for three weeks if suitably pampered.

Packaged and Canned Foods

These foods will provide the core of your provisioning for a sea passage. Everyone has their own preferences, of course, but I routinely stock up on the following items: dried fruits like dates, raisins, and apricots; nuts; lentils and beans of various types (pinto, kidney, navy, garbanzo or chick-peas, split peas, just to list a few); rice; and pasta (spaghetti, macaroni, noodles wide and narrow, penne regate, fussili, are some suggestions.) Other basics like flour (whole wheat, white, corn flour), cornmeal, yeast, baking powder, salt, herbs and spices, olive oil, butter, bread crumbs, crackers, peanut butter, honey, jam, syrup, sugar, coffee, tea, milk (dried or canned), and cereals round out the staples.

Canned foods are important, and many cruisers apparently subsist entirely upon them, a practice I hope to discourage with this book! A few suggestions from my list include: string beans, peas, spinach, asparagus, artichoke hearts, mushrooms, creamed and whole corn, garbanzo beans (chick-peas), kidney beans, beets, potatoes, yams, whole tomatoes, tomato paste, and fruits of your choice. Condiments make another useful addition to the galley, as they give variety to often used foods. Chutney, pickles, olives, mustard, horseradish, and your favorite sauces should be on your list.

Menu Plans for the Passage

Now that your veggie basket and food lockers are full, what are you going to do with all of it?

For any lengthy passage I make a menu plan, or chart. This makes organizing meals at sea a much easier task, especially when you are tired or you encounter rough conditions. I don't make a rigid plan, but I make a chart of all the various dishes I plan to prepare during the voyage depending on our palates, the expected sea conditions, and the availability of fresh foods. I always carry an adequate supply of canned goods just in case I don't feel like cooking or the conditions are too difficult. Include these in your menu plan so you will remember your alternatives. A menu plan also helps when you ask yourself, or your mate, "What shall we have for dinner?" And invariably they ask you in return, "What are the choices?" It can be fun for them to look at the list and make a choice! Then strike that meal from your plan (since you have used those provisions), so you won't choose it again. Using a menu plan also prevents you from having to eat the same thing the last three days of your trip!

After making a list of all dishes for which I have provisioned, including breakfasts, lunches, dinners, and snacks, I then make a chart for the anticipated number of days in the passage (plus extra days for safety margin) and fill it in from my menu list, repeating as necessary. We don't always have "lunch" at lunch or "breakfast" for breakfast, but that's basically how I categorize them. I also try to organize my plan so that we won't be eating potatoes three times a day.

Thus, my menu plan, or chart, is made. As a menu item is used, it is crossed off the chart so I can readily see what I have left in the locker. On a short passage this isn't so important, but on a long one of several weeks I find it quite worthwhile, and it can be fun both to make and to use. Below is a sample of a 28-day menu plan using recipes included in this book.

	Passage Menu Plan for 28 Days		
	BREAKFAST	**LUNCH**	**DINNER**
1	Cereal, bananas	Potato salad, orange	Spaghetti, green pepper sauce
2	Biscuits, eggs	Cabbage, carrot salad	Curried vegetables on rice
3	Cereal, bananas	Macaroni salad, orange	Potatoes, carrots, peas
4	Pancakes, eggs	Rice-fruit salad, raisins	Veggie Stew
5	Cereal, bananas	Cabbage, carrot salad	Lentils and veggies on rice
6	Cheese omelette	Potato salad, orange	Stir-fry veggies on noodles
7	Cereal, grapefruit	Marinated garbanzos	Minestroni
8	Biscuits, eggs	Rice-veggie salad	Mexican beans on macaroni
9	Cereal, grapefruit	Pasta salad	Chili potatoes, onions, green beans
10	Basted eggs on rice	Cole slaw, raisins	Spaghetti/basil-tomato sauce
11	Cereal	Potato salad, orange	Veggie Stew
12	Hash browns/basted eggs	Macaroni/tomato sauce	Mexican rice with avocado
13	Cereal	Marinated garbanzos	Macaroni-veggie casserole
14	Biscuits and eggs	Cole slaw, raisins	Mashed potatoes, peas, carrots
15	Cereal	Rice salad, apple	Mexican beans, cornbread
16	Pancakes	Potato salad	Curried Veggies on rice
17	Spanish Tortilla	Split pea soup	Spaghetti with tomato sauce
18	Cereal	Pasta salad	Biksemad
19	Biscuits, jam, honey	Lentil pate /crackers	Spinach noodles/mushrooms, veggies
20	Cereal	Cole slaw	Mexican rice, corn
21	Pancakes	Rice-fruit salad	Alubias or limas with can. spinach
22	Cereal	Potato salad	Potatoes, green beans, carrots
23	Cereal	Macaroni salad	Cheese-Chilies cornbread
24	Basted eggs on cornbread	Potato-leek soup	Spaghetti with tomato sauce
25	Biscuits, jam, honey	Macaroni/tomato sauce	Curry sauce on rice
26	Cereal	Rice-veggie salad	Macaroni-veggie casserole
27	Pancakes	Macaroni/tomato sauce	Sautéed potatoes with green beans
28	Biscuits and eggs	Potato salad	Rice, curried lentil/with veggies

Realities of Cooking At Sea

If you are embarking on a long passage, you probably already have made at least a few sea-trials that include preparing meals at sea. If not, do it! On a long passage, just the thought of getting out of the bunk, or going down below to cook, often can be discouraging enough, even before you try to light the cook stove, so a little practice and experience will give you confidence that you really can do it. After you have conquered a few gumption traps—or when you get hungry enough— you *will* decide to prepare something to eat. A little meditation or planning before you make your move to the galley can prevent a few minor disasters from occurring.

1. Adapt your menu to the sea conditions, giving careful thought to the necessary ingredients. Don't plan to make complicated sandwiches where you will have mayonnaise and mustard jars sitting vulnerably on the table while you wash the lettuce, slice the bread, cheese, and tomatoes, etc. Plain cheese sandwiches might be a better choice.

2. Map out in your mind where all the ingredients you will need are stowed, how you are going to get them out, and most importantly, where you will put them when you remove them from their safe nesting place. Once I lost a head of garlic after I put it on the counter top. The next large wave took it flying off into hiding (I found it weeks later in the book case behind a seldom used book). I have double sinks, and they are the best place to put any item that is a potential missile. On the top of my sturdy 40-inch square dinette table I have a 1" x 2" wooden cross piece, secured at each end with a small "C" clamp. I can move it inboard or outboard to "corral" small items and keep them from sliding into the radio or onto the sole. On the tabletop I usually place a damp dish towel that works wonders in most conditions, preventing plates, cups, small jars, utensils, and bowls from sliding. I also have several small canvas or acrylic covered flat cushions that I use in front of or behind objects to prevent them from moving. Lest you be put off by these precautions, I usually don't find them all necessary. However, I am cautious just out of habit, because it's that rogue wave that sneaks up after you've become complacent that causes your dinner to sortie. I will never forget the time I was motoring along a canal in the Sacramento Delta to pick up my friends in one of the small landing places. I had prepared a large pot of stew (which I thought to be secure on the stove), and the table was ready for supper as soon as they were aboard. A motor boat came speeding along close beside me, then proceeded to circle me twice, producing a ring of seas that caused *Sandpiper*

to gyrate as if she was in a Hula-Hoop. The stew went onto the carpet, the table's contents crashed on top of the stew, and all I could do was watch in horror as the cabin became a total disaster area. Of course it was illegal for them to go so fast as to "cause damage to other boats," but it still happened. Since then, I always try to be prepared for the worst.

3. With the items securely situated, and the cooking pot well fixed on the stove, you can begin whatever cleaning, chopping, and mixing of the ingredients is needed, placing them in the pot as they are ready. This is when it can become a gymnastic adventure, and you will do well to have chosen a simple one-pot recipe to prepare. I highly recommend a pressure cooker (I have two, a small one and a large one) because it has a tight, non-leaking, non-sliding lid, and because the cooking time is usually much shorter, making your attention and exposure time much shorter too. The larger the pot the better, since the food won't slosh out as easily. You can even fry foods down in there, steam vegetables on a rack, boil eggs, and if it's big enough, place several different dishes inside to cook at the same time.

4. Light the stove: Now, this may seem a simple task, but it isn't necessarily so. I began my cruising with a top-of-the-line kerosene stove. In harbor, it was fine: it didn't blacken my pots, it was easy enough to light, and except for when there was fuel rationing in 1973 and I couldn't get a permit to buy kerosene, it was reliable and inexpensive. However, at sea it proved to be a different matter. The problem was filling the cup with starter fluid to preheat the burner before lighting it. Even in a fairly smooth sea the alcohol sloshed out of the cup and down into the stove, and then it would flare-up at the sight of the match, which made me nervous. However, all the "experts" declared how safe kerosene stoves are, so I persevered for three years. In the Marquesas I even paid for a lesson from another enterprising yachtie on how to clean and repair the burners. I bought new burners; they were inferior and lasted only a year. Finally, in Australia I decided I would gladly risk blowing-up in one final explosion than slowly starving to death trying to cope with my "safe" kerosene stove, so I trashed it (no Aussie would have it) and changed to LP gas. What a relief! In a rough sea we have tea, coffee, and soups in an instant; my pots, ceiling, and towels stay clean; and I no longer have to carry bottles of alcohol and kerosene. For the last ten years I have been using "International Camping Gaz" bottles that are easy to stow, easy to change in a rough sea (as opposed to filling a kerosene stove with a funnel waving about in the back of the stove), and everywhere I have been lately (Europe and West Indies), they have been easy to get refilled.

5. Cook your food: Try to make the time-on-the-stove as short as possible. Do not leave a stove while food is cooking. Don't take the chance of losing your meal and having a sloppy mess to clean up, for you could also lose you boat because of a fire. A misbehaving stove, a rogue wave, an unsecured pot—or any number of unforeseen things—can really ruin your day and your cruise. I have never had a stove-accident at sea, but I know it could happen any time. So, I always station myself at the stove, even if there is only a well-secured and firmly closed pressure cooker on the burner. My galley is designed so that I can brace myself on the dinette table while working at the sink, counter top, or stove; or, when working on the table, I brace the other way around—against the sink's cabinet. If your boat is wider than mine, you probably will want to use a galley safety belt. I also can sit at the dinette table and watch the stove from there while taking a well-deserved rest. If everything is going well, I might even sneak another chapter from a good book.

6. Serve your meal: This might seem obvious, but if the sea is rough, be sure your crew is ready to receive it, hang on to it, or have a secure place to set it *before* you dish it out! Deep bowls usually work best, or in the worst conditions I use large mugs (even for cereal). Keep the cutlery simple—no knives as the food usually is already bite-size. Again, a dampened cloth on the cockpit seat helps prevent the bowls, cups, or plates from sliding as well as catching the spills. Obviously, it is best not to hand out several plates and bowls at once. Even an added beverage can cause a dilemma.

On a long passage we usually are able to sit down below at the table together to eat. Even in rough conditions, when the wind vane is steering and we are confident that there are no obstacles in our path, we enjoy this social event of the day. My table has substantial fiddles; so with dampened cloth, and something for the plates to "lean" against, we are able to eat and enjoy conversation with some light dinner music.

When sea conditions are reasonable, I can prepare most of the dishes in this book. Really, this does happen! But some people don't feel inclined to cook much at sea, and would rather stick to simple fare. There are many times when I serve peanut butter or cheese sandwiches, or in very rough seas, open canned foods and eat them *au natural*, but if at all possible I like to have a hot, nutritious meal at least once a day. I am lucky not to suffer from seasickness, but I do get the "hungries" especially at sea. My galley is excellently designed for preparing meals (thank you, Mr. Stephens). I find it sporting to try to produce something just a little bit unexpected to pass out the hatch to my dutiful crew, and he is always willing to stand watch extra time to allow this to happen.

I would like to add, though, that rough conditions are only a small portion of the normal cruising life. I think I have experienced more than my share: the 26 days across the Atlantic, often called the "milk-run," was more of a buttermilk run for *Sandpiper*. We rolled on and on, with seas breaking into the cockpit from time to time, as did Keith on the 27-foot sailboat *Reliance*, who was one day and a hundred miles in front of us; but somehow we both endured, and he, being a fanciful chef and singlehander, finally relented to the game of creative cooking-'n-rolling too. It was amusing listening to Keith on the SSB radio sharing his cooking successes-and-failures with other yachts on the same passage. It gave me encouragement to carry on. But, there have been many passages during which we could share lunch and dinner in the cockpit in civilized, pleasant conditions, and even set our wine glasses down between sips. Those are the times I remember best.

Cleanup Tips

There are several brands of dish detergent that work equally well in salt or fresh water. Joy seems to be the favorite in the United States, but I have bought other brands in Europe and the Caribbean that are similar and are easier on the skin. Rubber gloves are almost essential when you constantly use salt water and Joy. Without gloves my hands peel and become sore, especially under the nails. Your skin is very vulnerable when you are at sea, so you need to take special care to avoid open sores that can occur in damaged areas. A good, heavy hand cream can help. I have found A and D Ointment excellent for all types of skin irritations. I try to keep a small bowl of fresh water in the sink for rinsing salty hands when we come below.

I would like to add a comment regarding detergent: many incidents of "belly-runs" can be attributed to dishes not being rinsed well. So, with plenty of clean sea water around you, especially on passage, you should try to be particularly thorough in rinsing dishes. As a further precaution against stomach ailments, I often use a couple of drops of Clorox in the final fresh water rinse. With only one or two people aboard, you can't afford to get sick at sea!

Eating It In Rough Weather

During foul weather, it is especially important to maintain a good, nutritious diet. The added stress of a storm or rough seas, not to mention the added exercise you get just holding on, reefing sail, and steering the boat, uses much more of our energy (calories) than we might realize. This can cause fatigue and loss of appetite, which in turn causes you to feel even worse. So, it is important to plan for such events as rough seas and foul weather, and to have plenty of nutritious food available without any preparation.

Often you have warning about approaching unfavorable weather, so you can plan accordingly. If bad weather is expected, try to organize food so that it will be easy to reach and simple to prepare. Often I will cook a pressure cooker full of stew, beans, spaghetti with sauce, or a rice dish, early before the storm is due to arrive, so that we will have something ready-to-eat and which can be reheated if desired. Sandwiches can be made ahead, and will keep if well wrapped. They are very handy to pass out to the duty-crew who will usually welcome anything you can give them. Hard-boiled eggs are good sources of protein, easy to boil in sea water, and they will keep for a time. A thermos of your favorite hot drink is good to have, but be extremely careful filling the thermos with boiling liquid when the sea is rough. Scalding burns are dangerous and painful!

If your provisions include goodies and special treats that you hid in a locker prior to departure, this might be the time to move them to the top of the heap within easy reach. Peanuts, crackers, biscuits, dried fruit, chocolate bars, and granola bars are but a few items I try to save for this occasion. With foul weather, out come the goodies, making it a special occasion—almost. Instant beverages that can be used without hot water are also good to have handy. Cheese, fruit, or cereals make easy and nutritious "handouts." Some canned foods can be O.K. eaten just as they come out of the can. In fact, when it's really rough, almost anything that doesn't require something done to it is acceptable to us. Be sure your can-opener is handy and working well; it pays to buy the best one you can. It is a helpless feeling when you have a can of food in front of you and you can't get it open! If you provisioned with healthful foods, you won't have to worry about what you pluck out of the locker to eat. You should also remember to take your multivitamins and vitamin C, the anti-stress vitamin, so have them available.

When you've prepared your galley as much as you can for the coming situation, try to have a good rest and a good meal before things get too rough.

The storm will be over eventually, and you'll be proud of yourselves for being ready!

Securing the Galley

During the 23 years I have been living and cruising in *Sandpiper*, I have discovered a few "tricks" that make life on a small boat more pleasant.

I like to have everything function properly. I don't like rattles, squeaks, clanging halyards, bashing dinghies, things falling out of place, or any unnecessary noises, and I will immediately fix anything that I am able to fix. On our 35-day passage to the Marquesas I had provisioned and stowed everything well. But after using some of the canned goods from the locker, one night an annoying tink, ge-tink, tink, came from the depths of my main canned goods' locker. We each endured through one of our "sleep" periods, but finally it got the better of John, whom I found digging down to the bottom of the locker to find a small can of tomato paste melodically rolling in the extra space between two larger cans. Since then, I make sure everything is tightly packed into the locker with no chance to tink about.

For unwanted rattles and noises inside lockers and cabinets, I have a selection of small, soft, colorful acrylic-covered cushions about 12 inches square that I stuff into any areas that offer space for movement of articles to begin. My theory is: pack it tight, so nothing can start to move. These little cushions can be used later in the cockpit or bunk, or in any place where potential space needs filling. Make them soft so they can conform to the space where you need them for movement control. I believe it was Doris, on *Jolly II Roger,* who made little "pillows" filled with small Styrofoam balls (like those used in beanbag chairs) which she used to fill the empty space in the top of her freezer and refrigerator, helping maintain low temperatures.

Another "trick" that I have found helpful is the canvas (or acrylic) bag. I make them to fit many of my galley items that tend to otherwise get loose and rattle: pot lids, frying pan with its lid, the food mill with its parts, miscellaneous pots and their lids, and glass items that I like to use in port but don't want flailing about at sea. Socks work well for protecting wine bottles, wine glasses, and other miscellaneous glass bottles. Beyond the safety feature, the socks prevent unwanted clanking. Many captains don't believe in having any glass at all aboard, which I must agree is commendable, but I like a stemmed wine glass for that special dinner in harbor. With prudence, I have not broken any in my many years of cruising. I propose a toast!

Towels and rags, hot pads, and pot holders are also helpful in stopping noises created by movement. At sea I put them around my spice bottles, in drawers, and in shelf lockers where those little bottles or dishes are stored.

If the water pump in your galley sink has a spout that is high enough for pots or bottles to fit under, chances are that water dribbles out onto the counter top or into the outboard cupboards when the boat is heeling or rolling. This really annoyed me, so I fitted a short length of clear plastic tubing over the spout and led it into the sink. It is short enough that I can get almost anything I want under it for filling, yet long enough to prevent water from dripping outside the sink. Since it is flexible, it helps in cleaning the sink too. In port, it is easy to slip it off and save it for the next rough passage.

Sinks do become clogged from time to time, usually with a small piece of lettuce or spinach. A "plumber's friend," or plunger is invaluable. I found a small one with a short 10-inch handle, so it's easy to stow, and it does the job. It is also useful to unstop cockpit drains that becomes clogged with hair, leaves, saw dust, or small bits of lint. You might not use it often, but when you need it, it is a friend indeed. Bonus note: We also use it to place over the Sumlog impeller when pulling it out to clean—no geyser of water!

Have you ever heard snoring when no one was asleep? Look to your sinks. During certain sea conditions, my sink snores loudly enough to be annoying. I thought my sinks had some kind of design fault until I heard other skippers talking about their snoring sinks. My solution is simply to put rubber stoppers in each one during "vocal" conditions. Of course you could just close the sea cock to the sink, which isn't a bad idea either.

Keeping pots on the cooker can call for a bit of ingenuity when you are using a two-burner, un-gimbaled stove. I have not had much of a problem with this during the many "normal" passages I have made, since when settled down on a long tack, my large pots stay in place with only the stove's encircling railing and a couple of moveable crossbars secured tightly against the pan. I also have two small wedges that I slip under the lee side of the cooker when the angle of heel is enough to need them. Since my cooker is near the waterline, that works very well. However, on my downwind Atlantic passage, it was an entirely different story. I was unable to wedge the lee side of the stove to make it level, because we were rolling some 25° on either side every five seconds, so there was no "lee side." I was not accustomed to that! So, I secured the pots in place with anything fireproof that would completely fill the space: empty tin cans, metal cups, or even a small pan that fit in the space. It worked, and I was able to cook, with full attention to my pot while the stove was lit. This is the time for those one-pot meals done in the pressure cooker.

Some of My Favorite Things

The ship's cook has a difficult enough time producing a meal in a small boat at sea without having to endure an ill-equipped galley. Since space as well as the chef's disposition is a major consideration, it is worth a little thought in selecting the items that you put in the galley. Often we just snatch a few (or too many) things from our land-kitchen and try to stuff them into the wee galley lockers. Many of the things we choose are inappropriate in the boat's kitchen: that cute little pan that heats just two cups of milk for hot chocolate; the rotary egg-beater that rusts and ceases to turn; the "designer" canister set whose lids fly off—or rust on; and the many one-purpose utensils (olive snatchers, sugar tongs, nut choppers. . .) that take up prime space or get sifted to the bottom of the heap and are forgotten or lost.

I enjoy cooking ashore, and usually enjoy the challenges of cooking at sea. Many years ago I discovered the folly of selecting small, lightweight equipment just because my boat is small. I learned that you can cook small amounts of food in a large steady pot just as well as in a small pot. My large pots stay securely on the stove, whereas smaller ones slide about unless tethered.

Pans with proper fitting lids will cook or steam the food—not the galley, with the added bonus that the lids stay on the pot rather than sliding off when an unexpected lurch occurs. All of my pots and pans have good lids, many of which are interchangeable. The lids have large, sturdy handles that can be grabbed with a heavy hot-pad.

It is my belief that you should invest in the best pots and pans that you can afford. You will be rewarded with their long life, and you will have equipment you can depend upon and which will look good for many years. A few professional quality pots are better than an array of flashy, colorful, useless shapes that take up space and rust in your lockers.

Here is what I use in my galley: two saucepans (one 3½ quart and one 1½ quart) with high, straight sides, long sturdy handles, and tight fitting lids; and two skillets (a medium and a large), each with slanted sides, long handles and lids.

All of these are of heavy composite construction: a nontoxic, easy to clean, stainless steel inner lining; a copper middle layer for heat retention; and an aluminum outer layer for even dispersing of heat. Sounds expensive? Perhaps, but I have had these pots for 16 years and they still look new. And they have cooked a lot of good meals!

I used to have a large wok with ring stand for my stove, with two steaming "baskets" and a woven bamboo lid. I enjoyed using this equipment, but when the wok got a hole in its bottom, I never replaced it because of the space it consumed, and it was impractical to use at sea. Several years later in Spain, I bought a typical Spanish *sartén*, which is a large wok-type pan but with a flat bottom. It has high slanted sides, and sturdy handles on opposite sides of the pan. Although it is a light weight, inexpensive pan, I use it every day because it sits and stays on my stove without any pot-holders. It also doubles as a large salad bowl, a fruit and veggie bowl, and as a second lid (when turned upside down) over my Dutch oven. Because of its light construction it doesn't heat evenly or retain the heat as well as the heavier pans, but I love it anyway.

I have two pressure cookers. One is small, and it is the best pressure cooker I have ever seen. The brand name is "Perfect," and it is made in Germany. It has a bottom of copper sandwiched between stainless steel. I like it because there is no weight to fall off the top, its two safety valves work "perfectly," and the safety release does not explode into the overhead. The safety valve consists of a small stainless steel ball bearing housed in heavy rubber that flexes enough for dangerous excess pressure to be released. Everything comes apart for cleaning with ease. I use this pot almost every day, and at sea it is my main cooking utensil. I can use it for everything from boiling eggs to making bread. My second pressure cooker is large enough to put three or four small jars inside for "canning," and is perfect for a large pot of stew or making popcorn.

One important point: all of my pots and pans stack inside one another, so they take up much less space than otherwise. Bear this in mind when you go shopping for galley equipment.

A water, or tea kettle, that fits firmly on the stove is something in everyday use, so buy a good one. Take note of the arrangement of your stove's pot holders, for you should be able to turn the pouring spout to whatever position you want— depending on the tack you are on—so that the water doesn't slosh out. I like to leave plenty of water in my kettle, because the added weight helps keep it steady. A solid, heat-protected handle is important, and a long spout facilitates filling a thermos. At sea, I even boil eggs in my kettle.

There are other pieces of galley equipment that you will find useful. A large strong colander that will fit securely in your sink is handy not only for draining spaghetti and other pasta, but also as a dish-drainer, for draining washed vegetables and fruit, and as a holder for those items that you assemble for cooking a meal. Mine is made of heavy, brightly colored plastic, and still looks new after 16 years, even though it has been in constant use.

All chefs have their own preferences when it comes to knives and choppers. What you use isn't as important as keeping it sharp, so be sure to have a good whetstone on board. I believe that a dull knife—that requires vigorous sawing and pressure to cut something—is much more dangerous than a sharp, sure knife with which you can get the job done quickly and easily. A chopping or cutting board that will fit over your sink will provide extra counter top space. It can be used not only for slicing but also as a serving tray for onions, tomatoes, cucumbers, and such for those do-it-yourself sandwiches or salads. But do keep your cutting board scrupulously clean, and put it out in the sun for an hour from time to time to sanitize it. Wiping it "clean" with a contaminated dish rag or sponge is a sure ticket for food poisoning. A galley-goop hint: spread newspaper under and beside the chopping board to receive the peels, pits, and other material you will discard. Not only can you enjoy reading those little articles you missed when you bought the paper several months previously, but when you finish preparing your veggies and fruit you just roll it up with the biodegradable scraps inside. If you carefully omit all plastic and other non-biodegradable materials, you can deep-six it if you are far at sea, remembering that orange peels will float a long way and possibly onto someone's beach.

Maintaining Good Health at Sea: A Nutritious Diet

Those who have been vegetarians ashore will have no trouble maintaining good nutrition and a balanced diet at sea. A vegetarian diet is usually a healthful one, and vegetarians by nature are often interested in nutrition. We generally eat larger servings of salads, vegetables, lentils, grains, beans, nuts, and fruits—all the things that you can easily take on a small boat for a long passage. Since sailors are notoriously enthusiastic eaters, you shouldn't have any trouble obtaining complete nutrition from foods other than meat. You just have to eat larger quantities of the things you do eat, and you don't have to be too concerned about calories and fat if you are careful about your selection of food. Interestingly enough, over a period of time you will lose your cravings for the high calorie foods. You won't have to "diet."

For the non-vegetarian, the idea of planning meatless meals over a long period of time seems almost impossible. This is due to the habit of planning a meal by first choosing what meat to have. Turn things around. First, decide what vegetables you will cook; then choose something to go with the veggies—rice and lentils, perhaps potatoes or pasta. Or, plan to have a pasta main dish, then add a salad. Put all the items you want to cook out so you can see them, and start a little creative thinking. For example: rice or egg noodles with stir-fry veggies; spaghetti with tomato-vegetable sauce; potato and vegetable stew; curried vegetables on rice; or macaroni-vegetable loaf with cole slaw.

Protein, the nutrient that seems to worry new meatless diners, is found in many non-meat foods. You might be surprised to learn that some plant foods are as good a protein source as meat. There are many theories and ideas about how much protein we need each day, but lately the trend seems to be for a smaller amount than was previously thought necessary. Since protein isn't stored in the body, a regular daily intake is needed. There are many foods that are excellent sources of protein that will be new to you, and are delicious and well suited for a small cruising boat. Many of the new soy products are not only very tasty, but have a long shelf life, are easy to stow, versatile, and easy to prepare. Tofu, soy milk powder, soy flour, soy cheeses, and Textured Vegetable Protein (TVP) of various shapes and flavors are items I always include in my provisions. They are all excellent sources of protein. And because you are not eating meat, probably you can eat some of the other high protein foods such as eggs and cheese, which you previously avoided because of the cholesterol and fat they contain.

Cruising boats generally spend far more time at anchor or moored than on long passages. And in almost every country, tropical island, or city that you visit, you will be able to find beautiful fresh fruit and vegetables. Shopping expeditions to the local farmer's market can entertain the whole crew (and they can help to carry your purchases back to the dinghy). Luckily, many places offer produce that is grown without insecticides; and although they may not look as "glossy" as those in the supermarkets at home, their flavor is exceptional. These markets are a shopper's paradise: What a pleasure to select your food from such a kaleidoscopic display. The biggest problem most of us have is buying too much! Eating healthful foods is not at all difficult with so many enticements.

It is not within the scope of this book to list the nutritional specifics of each food, nor is it a text book on individual requirements. There are many good books on the subject of nutrition, and I think you should have at least one of these aboard to which you can refer. Maintaining good health on a cruising boat is perhaps easier than you would think: we aren't normally exposed to the many unhealthful foods that one finds living ashore, and the everyday temptations to eat fast foods, ice creams, fancy cakes and pies, cokes, and potato chips are swept away by setting sail seaward. Your pleasures will be fulfilled in a myriad of other ways.

Why A Meatless Galley Cookbook?

As a vegetarian, often I have been approached by the chief cooks of other cruising yachts asking for ideas on meatless meals. "The doctor said my husband has to cut out meat. I don't know what on earth to fix for dinner!" Or, "My refrigeration has broken down, and here we are a thousand miles from a butcher shop. I had to give away a freezer-full of meat; now what am I going to eat?" Many people just want to cut down on the amount of meat they eat, yet don't feel as if they have had a decent meal if they don't have meat. What is a hardy, satisfying dish they can prepare?

Thus, the purpose for this book is to share with my friends some of the simple recipes for the dishes that they have enjoyed on my boat, and to give to other small boat sailors ideas that might help make their passages and anchorages something really special, as mine have been.

I don't have a refrigerator, and I don't have the worries of maintaining one. Nor do I spend the better part of my day searching an unfamiliar town for a palatable piece of meat. So, the benefits you derive from a meatless galley are more than the salubrious feeling you will have every day, but also the freedom from everything that buying, keeping, and cooking meat entails.

Planning and preparing meatless meals today has become much easier and more interesting that it was several years ago. I discovered specialty shops in many small towns in Spain where foods grown without chemicals were sold, along with long-life packaged tofu, seitan (wheat-meat), fabulous TVP products, nut-milks, and many more products that were new to me. In the Caribbean I was surprised to discover a large company that makes all natural, non animal foods, the best I have ever used. Besides the granola, instant soy milk powder, TVP, and other dried foods, I found several delicious pre-made foods available: lentil patties; soya-chick, which has the texture and taste of chicken breasts; and many other tasty non-animal products. Their sesame or oatmeal cookies are temptingly delicious and free of cholesterol or animal fat.

The Specifics: Measurements and Ingredients

As for the measurements, ingredients, and number of servings for each recipe, I would like to add a few comments. The measurements and ingredients are certainly not rigid, except in the recipes for breads and perhaps some of the sauces. To me the fun of vegetarian cooking is being able to experiment with the many different foods one encounters from country to country—incorporating new vegetables into your favorite dish. Only by trying them will you discover a new taste treat, and this variety is what breaks the monotony in your meals. My best meals are typically made when "I don't know what to fix for dinner." Then I pile whatever veggies that I have on the table and start concocting.

I haven't stated the number of servings for most recipes, because it depends on who is eating it. Hungry sailors like to eat. For the most part, the proportions in these recipes are those that I use to cook for the two of us: one ravenous sailor and a more moderate lady skipper (with a spare serving for the singlehander who just *happens* to drop by at meal time). We rarely have leftovers, and when we do they make good snacks.

Over the years I have cut down considerably on the use of fat—oils, butter, and margarine—and have found that it does not detract from the flavor of most dishes at all (although there are some things that just taste so much better with butter!). Then I found that half the amount of butter will usually give the same enhancement. I encourage you to do the same in the interest of health. I also use egg substitutes when I can, and I use salt rarely and sparingly.

Nutritional information for the recipes is not included in this book, because of the wide variation in the foods that I have found around the world. Since I invite you to vary and alter a recipe to suit your tastes, such figures would be inaccurate. Consult a book on nutrition if you need to calculate figures for the ingredients that you use.

It's time for the crew "to lash and stow, and pipe the cooks to the galley!"

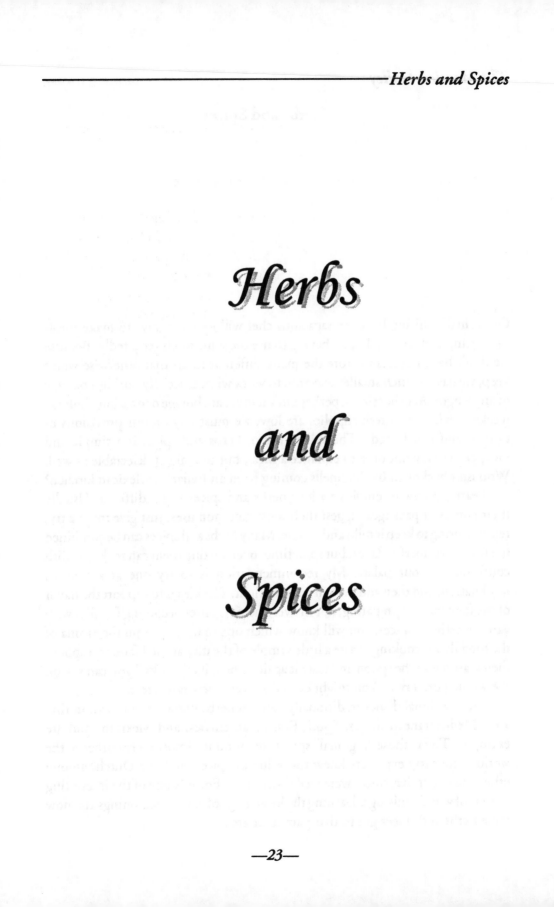

Herbs

and

Spices

Herbs and Spices

On a small cruising boat the sagacious chef will look for ways to make meals interesting and savory, despite having to use the same foods repeatedly. Because we don't have freezers to store the many different foods that otherwise won't keep, we have a much smaller selection to work with, especially during a passage of any length. At other times, perhaps in a remote anchorage or on a long holiday weekend when our fresh supplies are low, we must rely on our provisions of canned and dried foods. The skilled use of herbs and spices is a simple and inexpensive way not only to enhance a meal, but to make it delectable as well. Who isn't beckoned by the smells coming from an Italian or Mexican kitchen?

Learning how to employ various herbs and spices is not difficult. Usually their bottles or packages suggest their most common uses. Just give them a try, remembering to keep it mild and simple. Many herbs and spices can be combined to create a wonderful flavor, but sometimes over-mixing them can make the dish confusing to your palate. My recommendation is to try one at a time in moderation, and then add more if it seems right. The idea is to support the flavor of the food you are preparing, not to overwhelm it! After becoming familiar with various herbs or spices, you will know which one to use just from the aroma of the food that is cooking. Taste a little sample of the unseasoned food in a spoon, then season it in the spoon and taste it again. Then, if it "works," you can season the whole pot. Try it. You might even discover a new taste treat.

Most regional dishes traditionally contain herbs known and grown in that area: Mediterranean dishes, South East Asian curries, and Mexican food are examples. Today those "regional" spices are found in almost every corner of the world. The early explorers knew the value of spices, and the Dutch, among others, saw to it that spices were well distributed. For me, one of the interesting aspects of world cruising is learning the local usage of various seasonings and how these herbs and spices got to that particular area.

When cooking with leafy herbs, add them during the last 5 or 10 minutes of cooking; don't boil them hard or their delicate flavors will be lost. On the other hand, seeds and spices usually can be added earlier and cooked longer to bring out their flavor.

In order to have the true and full flavor of your herbs and spices, don't store them over your stove, where it is hot! It's a good idea to mark the date of purchase on the bottle or package so that they can be discarded when they become too old and lose their characteristics. It is such a small expense to keep them current so that you can rely on their flavors.

The following list contains only the more common herbs and spices and the ones used in recipes in this book.

ANISE

Anise is a long pale green or light brown seed which tastes and smells like licorice. It is native to the Middle East, and is used in soups, salads, cookies and breads. In Spain and France they use it in liqueurs.

BASIL or SWEET BASIL

Used in salads, stews, tomato dishes, and sauces, basil is an aromatic herb that has a fresh and minty flavor. It is often used in combination with oregano and thyme in Italian dishes. I have kept a small plant on my boat and "harvested" it regularly to use for seasonings. My Italian friend hangs basil plants in her house as a mosquito deterrent. It is decorative and fragrant, and easy to grow.

BAY LEAF, OR LAUREL

Bay leaf is one of the essential ingredients of Herb Bouquet or Bouquet Garni which consists of parsley, thyme, and bay leaf. Bay leaf sometimes is used in custards and milk puddings to impart a modified almond flavor. Bay leaves are used in cooking pulses, soups, marinades, and sauces.

CARAWAY SEEDS

These are the little seeds used in rye bread. They are also good for flavoring sauces, curries, salads, dressings, and grains. Add them to a basic white sauce to serve over steamed cabbage.

CELERY SEED

A tiny, potent seed used in dressings and stuffings, stews, soups and casseroles. I like it in potato salad when I don't have fresh celery.

CHERVIL

Chervil imparts a savory flavor to boiled potatoes when added near the end of the cooking time. It is used in the same way as parsley for flavoring soups, savories and salads.

CHIVES

Chives give a subdued onion flavor when snipped over salads and in *au gratin* dishes. They are easily grown in a small pot and continue to grow as you snip from the top. They are good flavoring when stirred into cottage cheese, cream cheese, and sour cream.

CINNAMON

Cinnamon is the bark of a tree grown in Grenada in the West Indies, as well as in Malaysia. It is used in many dishes around the world from cinnamon toast to curries, Christmas sweets to Mexican beans.

CLOVES

Cloves are the dried flower buds of a tree found in the tropics. The limbs of the trees are very flexible, so that harvesting them is a matter of bending the branches to pluck the cloves. They are used in Indian and West Indian cooking, as well as in fruits and desserts all around the world. Cloves are a major flavoring in toothpaste and some cosmetics. They make a wonderful air-sweetener.

CORIANDER

The green leaves are used fresh as an herb, and the little pale brown seeds are used as a spice. It is used in breads, soups, and sauces.

CUMIN

Called *comino* in Spanish, it is a small seed used in beans, soups, gravies, and Mexican dishes. It is a main ingredient in chili powder and curry powder. It's flavor is best when the seeds are rubbed briskly between the palms of your hands, then fried for a few seconds in hot oil before you add the rest of the ingredients.

CURRY POWDER

Curry powder is a mixture of many spices, depending on the area from which the dish you are preparing originates. Some of the spices used in curry powder are turmeric, cumin, coriander, cayenne, fennel (or anise), cardamom, ginger, mustard seeds, and fenugreek. Roast or fry the curry powder for a minute or two before adding the vegetables.

DILL

Dill is one of my favorite herbs, and one that I have not found in very many places around the world. It is a hardy plant which propagates itself every year. It gives a fresh flavor to many foods, including salads, soups, dressings, vegetables, and even bread. It is a good addition to cottage cheese, and, of course, it is used in making dill pickles.

FENNEL

The seeds of the fennel are mainly used for flavoring in sauces and soups. They are also used for flavoring breads and some sweets. The entire plant is used as a vegetable, either cooked or raw, and is good mixed with other vegetables. Fennel keeps well on the boat, and the little green "hairs" are good chopped on top of dishes for flavoring.

FENUGREEK

Fenugreek seeds are used in making certain curry powders. Use them to make your own curries by sautéing them in a little oil along with cumin, mustard seeds, and cayenne. The seeds sprout well, the sprouts being good in salads and sandwiches. Ground fenugreek seeds are good flavorings for grains and bean soups.

MARJORAM

A very useful herb, used in soups, salads, dressings, sauces, stuffings, and breads. It is often mixed with oregano and basil in making Italian sauces.

MINT

Shred fresh mint on salads, or sprinkle over cooked potatoes, rice, peas, beans, or lentils. Use a couple of fresh mint leaves in tea for a refreshing drink, or make mint tea of itself. Mint is also used crushed in lemon juice for a mint sauce. My grandmother always had an abundance of mint growing in her yard, and I don't remember her serving iced tea without a sprig of mint added on top. And how about Mint Juleps?

MUSTARD SEED

This little black seed is used all over the world and is an excellent for adding zing to vegetables, sauces, sandwiches, and curries. The plant makes a good raw salad, or cooked as a vegetable. We have all heard of mustard plasters for aches and congestion. The condiment "mustard" is made from the seeds.

NIGELLA SEEDS

These are tiny, hard, black seeds (often called onion seeds). They impart a distinctive flavor to curries, and should be fried until they pop—along with other seeds you use—when making your curry sauce. You'll find them in Indian spice shops.

NUTMEG

In each country I visit around the world, I discover another use for nutmeg. The nutmeg tree is a large, beautiful tree with pale yellow fruit which opens from the bottom, revealing a bright red nut hanging inside. The red covering on the "nut," after it is removed and dried, is called mace. The fruit of the nutmeg is used to make delicious jams, jellies, and syrup. The hard covering over the inside nut is salvaged and used for ground cover in gardening. The inside nut is grated for "nutmeg." I never knew it could be so delectable until I started grating it fresh for each use. It is used in Indian curries, puddings, cream sauces, sweet breads, peas, beans, and in Holland I learned to use it in spinach. Eggnog and many milk drinks use nutmeg. It helps prevent food fermentation.

OREGANO

Probably the most well-known herb used in Italian cooking, it is commonly used in pizza, spaghetti, and tomato sauces.

PAPRIKA

Paprika is of the pepper family. It is a sweet red pepper, dried, ground to a beautiful red powder and used to flavor soups, stews, eggs, sauces, dressings, and curries. It adds color when sprinkled on top of potato salad, deviled eggs and the like. In Europe, paprika can either be sweet paprika or hot paprika, the latter also called cayenne. It is the main spice in many Hungarian dishes. In my opinion the best paprika comes from Hungary.

PARSLEY

Parsley comes in many different varieties around the world. It is used as a garnish for many foods, including orange slices, lemon wedges and drinks. I keep a large jar of dried parsley on board and use it in stews, soups, butter sauces, and potato salad. It is a breath sweetener, and contains significant amounts of vitamin C.

SAFFRON

Saffron is a little flower of the crocus family. The deep orange threads are expensive, and in the United States it was usually found in a pharmacy; however, lately I have seen saffron in some supermarkets. The threads are usually soaked in warm water for a few minutes before use in a recipe. They add a rich flavor and a golden color to grains, sauces, teas, vegetables, noodles, and breads. It is a potent fabric dye.

SAGE

One of the things I liked most about Thanksgiving and Christmas was my mother's stuffing: half corn bread and half stale bread, and lots of sage along with the other ingredients. Sage is also good in cheese dishes, and is an excellent flavoring herb for TVP and other soy products. You can even make sage tea and it is also good in hot milk.

THYME

Thyme, called *tomillo* in Spanish, is a little green herb which I use often. It is good in stews, in tomato dishes, salads, and dressings.

TURMERIC

A root of the ginger family, turmeric is found in the markets of many Caribbean islands where it is sold alongside fresh ginger. It is golden in color, and you will find your fingers also golden when you slice it, so beware. Turmeric gives yellow coloring to curries and rice. It can be used as a potent dye, which you will discover if you get it on your clothes or dish towels. The flavor is subtle and bland.

VANILLA

The vanilla bean originates in the tropics and makes a perfect flavoring for sweet foods and drinks. It is best if you boil the whole vanilla bean in water to extract the flavor. I sometimes put a piece of the bean in my coffee grounds. You can also extract the flavor by putting the whole bean in a well-stoppered glass "tube" filled with rum or unflavored brandy, and allow it to soak until the flavor is extracted. It is used in many dishes from puddings, frostings and candies to ice cream and drinks. Try adding a few drops on the coffee grounds next time you make coffee.

Herb Substitutes

The following herbs can be substituted one for another:

Basil	for	Oregano
Caraway	for	Anise
Celery seed	for	Minced celery tops
Chervil	for	Parsley
Chervil	for	Tarragon
Fennel	for	Anise
Fennel	for	Tarragon
Oregano	for	Marjoram
Sage	for	Thyme

When using fresh herbs in place of dry, double or triple the amount of fresh.

Spice Substitutes

Nutmeg	for	Mace
Tonka beans (extract)	for	Vanilla beans (extract)

Allspice: equal parts of cinnamon, cloves, nutmeg, chili peppers, and cayenne.

"HUSH PUPPIES"

Along the Gulf Coast of Florida, Alabama, Mississippi, Louisiana, and Texas, the "fish-fry" was very popular when I was growing up. Everybody including children and dogs showed up at the beach to check-out the fishermen's catch-of-the-day. Often as not, a big fire would be built under large pots full of oil, one of the favorite vessels being made from a 55-gallon drum slit down the middle, one of the halves turned on its side and propped up over the fire. Some people even welded legs on them. Rough tables held trays of corn meal, a bowl of beaten eggs, flour—all for battering the fish— plates of sliced onions, tomatoes, salt and pepper, a keg of iced tea and one of lemonade, and plenty of brown wrapping paper, or newspaper, for serving the fish. Several men cleaned and prepared the various kinds of fish while a couple of men, aproned with clean white dish towels, tended to the cooking. The fish were dipped first in egg, then either cornmeal or flour, depending on the type of fish, then fried to crispy brown. Of course the dogs centered their attention on the cooks, some dogs having better manners than others. When the cooks had been pestered enough, they made little balls of corn meal, flour, and a little egg, then tossed them in the deep hot fat to fry along with the fish. Taking out these little balls, which now smelled and tasted like fish, they tossed them a fair distance away, saying to the dogs "Hush puppies!"

In many restaurants today, especially in Texas, you will find Hush Puppies as well as fried okra on the menu as an appetizer. They are also eaten with soups and stews. Since they are not cooked with the fish, they won't have a fish flavor. They are a very popular vegetarian appetizer (or just a snack) when served with dips of barbecue sauce, or spicy mayonnaise. Here is my version of Hush Puppies:

Hush Puppies

1 cup coarse yellow corn meal
1 cup flour
2 teaspoons baking powder
1/2 teaspoon salt
1 egg, beaten
2 tablespoons oil
milk to make stiff dough
oil for frying

optional:
small chopped onion
chopped green pepper
chili powder or cayenne
cumin seeds

1. Mix the cornmeal, flour, salt, and baking powder in a medium-sized bowl. If using chili powder or other dry herbs or spices, mix them into the flour and cornmeal.

2. Make a hole in the center, break in the egg and beat the eggs with a fork. Add the oil. Mix only lightly.

3. Add just enough milk to make a dough stiff enough to form balls about the size of ping-pong balls.

4. Mix in the onions, green peppers, or other optional ingredients, stirring as little as possible.

5. Fry in hot oil until golden brown. Drain on absorbent paper.

Little Cheese Melties

grated cheddar cheese
green pepper, thinly sliced in rings
brown onion, thinly sliced in rings
tomato, thinly sliced
French bread sliced in thin rounds, or
sliced bread, quartered
mayonnaise
butter

These are best done in a broiler; however, I have cooked them in a very heavy skillet.

1. Spread each small piece of bread with a little butter or mayonnaise. Then add some grated cheese, a slice of onion, a slice of tomato, and finally a slice of green pepper. Top with a little sprinkle of cheese.

2. Place under broiler to toast slowly so that the cheese melts through the veggies. Serve hot.

If you use a skillet, spread a very thin coat of butter on the bottom of the bread. Cook very slowly to melt the cheese.

For variation, use only cheese and onion, or pepper and cheese.

Hummus

1 cup garbanzo beans (chick-peas)
2 whole lemons
2 bay leaves (laurel)
2 tablespoons olive oil
4 cloves garlic, minced
1¹/₂ cups fresh mint, finely chopped
juice of 1 lemon
1 tablespoon tamari
pepper

1. Soak the garbanzo beans (chick-peas) overnight or for 8 to 10 hours. Drain.
2. In a saucepan, put garbanzo beans, lemon juice and peel of 2 lemons, bay leaves and enough water to cover beans a couple of inches.
3. Simmer 2 hours (alternatively, cook in pressure cooker for about 1 hour) until beans are tender.
4. Drain and save the liquid, discarding the lemon peel and bay leaves.
5. Mash the beans, adding olive oil and garlic, mint, lemon juice, and some of the cooking liquid to make a smooth paste. Season with tamari and pepper. (You can use a blender if available).

Hummus is equally good as a dip or a spread. I like to make a tray filled with fresh raw vegetables cut to bite-size pieces and a bowl of hummus placed in the center for dipping. The assortment might include: cherry tomatoes; carrots and celery, cut into fingers; cauliflower broken into florets; green pepper and red onions, sliced into rings; whole small mushrooms (or large ones, quartered); zucchini sliced into rounds; and cucumber slices. As a spread, use hummus on toasted whole-wheat bread squares. Hummus is also good as a basic spread for sandwiches such as tomato and lettuce.

Marinated Artichoke Hearts

I spent six years in Spain, mostly near Barcelona where artichokes grow. They are the best I have ever had and very inexpensive. The small ones are especially tender and you can eat the whole thing, thistle and all. The larger ones are tender too, and I used the hearts often in salads. Also, you can scrape the cooked "meat" off the leaves and use it to make dips, both hot and cold.

For marinated artichoke hearts, you can either cook fresh artichokes, then carefully remove the hearts; or you can use the canned or bottled ones.

artichoke hearts
olive oil
garlic
salt and pepper
lemon juice

1. Crush several cloves of garlic into enough olive oil to cover artichoke hearts. Add salt and pepper, mix well.
2. Pour oil mixture over artichoke hearts and allow to sit several hours.
3. Place the slightly drained hearts on a plate, and squeeze lemon juice on top.

In Spain, "Tapas" are served at every bar. The selection might include: olives, both green and black; artichoke hearts, marinated mushrooms, and almonds. Each person is given a tiny fork, and often a small plate, to pick and choose.

Marinated Champignons

1 bottle or can button mushrooms, drained
¼ cup olive oil
juice of 1 lemon
pinch of oregano or basil

Make a marinade with the olive oil, lemon juice, and herbs. Pour it into the drained jar of mushrooms. Let stand for flavors to blend. Serve at room temperature.

Carrot Spread

1 cup grated carrots
1 onion, grated or finely chopped
1 green pepper, finely chopped
1 teaspoon fresh ginger, finely chopped
2 tablespoons wine vinegar
mayonnaise
freshly ground pepper

1. Mix the finely chopped vegetables in a bowl.
2. Add vinegar, then stir in enough mayonnaise to make a spreadable mixture, to your taste. Season with pepper.

Serve this spread with crackers for hors d'oeuvres, or spread on bread or toast for sandwiches. It is also good for stuffing celery.

I like to make my appetizers as healthful as the rest of my meal. I think they should be planned as a part of the menu, not as an add-on or afterthought. I try to avoid crisps, chips, and other packaged cocktail tidbits. Although they taste good, they are full of chemicals, unhealthful ingredients, and "empty calories." In addition, they are expensive, take up a lot of space in a small boat, and are very habit forming. So I don't tempt myself by filling my lockers with those crinkly packages, but try instead to keep alternatives in their place.

Refried Bean Rissoles

1 small onion, chopped fine
2 large cloves garlic
¼ teaspoon salt
1 teaspoon marjoram
1 teaspoon Worcestershire Sauce
West Indian Hot Sauce
1 cup refried beans
flour to make dough
1 round teaspoon baking powder
rolled oats
West Indian farine (cassava flour)
oil for frying

1. Finely chop onion and garlic. Put in a mixing bowl.
2. Break an egg over the onion and garlic and beat with a fork until a bit bubbly.
3. Add salt and marjoram, Worcestershire Sauce and a drop or two of West Indian Hot Sauce (or Tobasco or hot taco sauce).
4. Stir in refried beans and enough flour to make a dough light enough to stir in baking powder.
5. Make a mixture of about half farine (cassava flour) and half oats.
6. Roll large spoonfuls of dough in the farine-oat mixture.
7. Fry in small amount of oil.

These rissoles, or little fried cakes, are so delicious. Alison of the South African yacht "Abgwe" brought them for an evening sundowner party. They also make a good addition to dinner or lunch.

Mt. Hartman Bay, Grenada, West Indies. March 3, 1995

Salads

and

Dressings

Rice Salad

2 cups rice–already cooked and cold
1 small green or red pepper, chopped
(or a combination of both)
1 green onion, thinly sliced
1 tomato, finely chopped
1/2 cup corn
1 cucumber, chopped
1 stalk celery, diced
2 or 3 red radishes, chopped
1/2 teaspoon basil
lemon or vinegar dressing
white pepper

Mix all of the ingredients. Serve cold.

Carrot and Pineapple Salad

4 to 6 medium-sized carrots, grated
1 small can of crushed pineapple, drained
1 handful raisins
mayonnaise or sour cream to desired consistency
salt and pepper to taste

Mix all of the ingredients in a large salad bowl. Season with salt and pepper. If possible, chill before serving.

Carrot Salad I

2 carrots, shredded
1 raw beet, shredded
wedge of cabbage, thinly sliced or shredded
1 green onion, finely sliced
green pepper, cut in thin rings
1 cup yoghurt
juice from 1/2 lemon
white pepper
dill

Arrange the shredded or thinly sliced veggies on individual salad plates—cabbage on the bottom, carrots, then the onion rings and green pepper rings around the top. Mix the yoghurt, lemon juice and freshly ground pepper to make a dressing. Pour over the salad. Add a sprinkle of dill for variation.

Carrot Salad II

carrots, grated
green onions, thinly sliced
radishes, thinly sliced
cabbage, thinly sliced
lemon juice (or vinegar)
oil
pepper

Mix all the vegetables and place servings on individual salad plates. Drizzle the lemon juice and oil on top. Pepper to taste.

Carrot and Cabbage Salad

cabbage, shredded
carrots, shredded
green onions, thinly sliced
green pepper, sliced in rings
lemon

Place the carrots, cabbage and green onion on salad plates. Put the green pepper rings on top, and squeeze the lemon juice on top of everything.

Cole Slaw

1 cup grated carrots
3 cups cabbage, finely chopped
1 tablespoon onion, finely diced
1 green pepper, finely diced
1/4 cup vinegar
1 teaspoon sugar or honey
1/4 cup mayonnaise
freshly ground white pepper

Put all of the vegetables in a bowl. Mix the sugar with the vinegar and pour over the salad. Stir in the mayonnaise. Mix well. Add white pepper. Chill.

You can vary the dressing by using juice of a lemon and yoghurt in place of the sugar, vinegar and mayonnaise.

You can also change the flavor by adding a sprinkle of dill.

Instead of mayonnaise, try using yoghurt. Or make a sour cream dressing: the juice of one lemon added to one small can of evaporated milk. Let sit until thickened.

Fruit Cole Slaw

1/2 head of cabbage, more or less
2 bananas, sliced
1 cup pineapple pieces
1/3 cup pineapple juice
1/3 cup cherries (optional)
3 to 4 heaping tablespoons mayonnaise or sour cream
1/3 cup shredded coconut
1 tablespoon sugar

Chop the cabbage into small bits and put it in a large salad bowl. Add the other ingredients, leaving the mayonnaise until last. Mix thoroughly and chill if possible before serving.

If you like cherries and have them, they make a good and colorful addition.

Mayonnaise

Making your own mayonnaise isn't difficult, and you will know it is fresh and without additives. You don't have to use a blender or an electric mixer. Instead, use a fork with one or two cloves of peeled garlic stuck onto the tines. The garlic makes an effective "beater" and at the same time imparts a pleasant flavor to the mayonnaise.

1 egg yolk
1/2 teaspoon salt
2 tablespoons lemon juice or vinegar
1/8 teaspoon dry mustard
dash of freshly ground black pepper corns
3/4–1 cup salad oil

1. Combine and beat thoroughly the egg yolk, salt, lemon juice, mustard, and pepper.
2. Slowly—drop by drop at first—beat in the salad oil, beating constantly. Continue until all of the oil is added and the mixture emulsifies. Use more oil for a thicker mixture.

Hot Indonesian Rice Salad

1 cup brown rice
2 cups water
4 tablespoons sesame oil
juice of 2 limes or lemons
1 clove garlic, crushed
2 dried red chilies, seeded and crushed
2 tablespoons soy sauce or tamari
1-2 tablespoons honey
2 tablespoons wine vinegar
3 green onions, thinly sliced
1 cup pineapple pieces in juice
1 cup bean sprouts
2 stalks celery, sliced
1/4 cup raisins
1/4 cup unsalted peanuts
1/4 cup cashew nuts, toasted
1 small red pepper, cored and sliced
pepper

1. Cook the rice in water by usual method.
2. Place the oil, lime or lemon juice, garlic, chilies, soy sauce, honey, vinegar, and salt and pepper in a large bowl and mix well.
3. Add the hot rice and remaining ingredients and mix well. Check the seasoning.

Serve hot or cold.

This is a dish that I found on the Indonesian "rijstafel" in Holland. It looks like an involved dish to make, but don't be discouraged by the list of ingredients. Assemble everything and then you will find it is an easy and interesting dish to prepare.

Macaroni Salad

1¹/2 cups salad macaroni
2 tablespoons onion, finely chopped
green pepper, chopped
1 small carrot, finely chopped
radishes, thinly sliced
1 stalk celery
¹/2 cucumber, quartered then sliced
parsley or dill
mayonnaise
¹/2 lemon
white pepper

1. Bring ample water to boil in a sauce pan. Sprinkle in the macaroni, and cook as directed on package. Wash the cooked macaroni, allow it to drain, then put it in a bowl to cool.
2. Add the veggies, herbs, and pepper, and mix well.
3. Squeeze the lemon juice over the macaroni mixture, mixing again.
4. Mix in mayonnaise, salt and pepper to taste.

You can also add a chopped boiled egg, and put slices of another boiled egg on top to garnish.

For a change, use curried mayonnaise in pasta and potato salads. Just add 1 teaspoon of curry powder to 4 tablespoons of mayonnaise. Curried mayonnaise is also good on sliced tomatoes, on hard boiled eggs, and as a dip for raw vegetables like cauliflower, celery, cherry tomatoes, and green pepper rings. Try it as a dip for chilled cooked artichokes.

Marinated Garbanzo Beans

2 cups cooked garbanzo beans (chick peas)
2 cloves garlic, minced
1 teaspoon chopped fresh thyme
(or 1/2 teaspoon of dried thyme)
1 tablespoon tamari
3 tablespoons fresh lemon juice
3 tablespoons olive oil
1/2 tablespoon freshly ground pepper
tomato wedges for garnish

Combine all ingredients except tomatoes. Allow to marinate in refrigerator if you have one, for at least one hour before serving, preferably overnight. Garnish with tomatoes and serve on lettuce.

Green Bean Salad

1 pound green beans
1 red onion, thinly sliced
marinade:
2 lemons
1/4 cup oil (olive oil is best)
1/4 cup water
2 cloves garlic, crushed and chopped
1/2 teaspoon salt
freshly ground black pepper

1.   Steam fresh green beans for 5 to 10 minutes, or use canned beans if fresh ones are not available.
2.   Mix the juice of 2 lemons, oil, water, garlic, and salt and pepper to make the marinade.
3.   Add the onions to the green beans, then mix in the marinade. Let stand for 15 or 20 minutes to allow the flavors to blend.

Macaroni Salad with Green Olives

2 cups elbow macaroni
2/3 cup green olives
2/3 cup yoghurt
freshly ground black pepper

1. Cook the pasta as directed on the package.
2. Drain, put in a bowl. Add the olives and a teaspoon or so of the juice.
3. Stir in the yoghurt and the freshly ground pepper.

This is an incredibly simple dish to prepare, but it is very popular, especially in Spain where the olives are so abundant and tasty. Spanish sailors joke that the holding ground in their harbors is so poor due to the quantity of olive pits on the bottom!

Cucumber Salad

2-3 cucumbers
1/2 teaspoon salt
pepper

1. Score the cucumbers by dragging a fork down the sides.
2. Thinly slice or shred the cucumbers and put in a container. Add salt.
3. Let stand in a cool place (refrigerate if possible) for several hours.
4. With your hands, squeeze the slices of cucumber and discard as much liquid as possible.
5. Put in a serving dish. Pepper to taste.
6. Serve as a side dish, on salads, in sandwiches, or as a relish.

This is really best if chilled for several hours (well, sometimes you might have ice). However, it is completely acceptable at room temperature. Since lettuce doesn't keep very well in the heat, plain sliced cucumber makes a good crunchy addition to sandwiches, even peanut butter sandwiches!

Oli-Oil

2 cloves garlic
2-4 tablespoons olive oil
salt, pepper

1. In a wooden mortar, or a wooden salad bowl, crush the garlic with a wooden pestle using a pounding motion. If you don't have one, use a large wooden spoon.

2. While pounding the garlic, add olive oil little by little, making a paste, then continue adding the oil, mixing well. The mixture will become creamy. Season to your taste.

This is a Catalan version that I learned from the baker's wife in Port Aiguadolç, Sitges, near Barcelona. She served it on boiled potato wedges sprinkled with finely chopped parsley.

If you make half the amount of oli-oil directly in your wooden salad bowl, adding a little lemon juice while pounding the garlic, then add lettuce, tomato wedges, sliced cucumbers, green pepper rings and perhaps red onion rings, you will have your dressing already made.

My favorite meal to prepare for a party is a salad "buffet." Since my boat is very small, all of my entertaining is done in the cockpit. I like to make seven or eight salads, keeping them cold if possible. I have found that zip-lock bags store the salads very well, they are sanitary, and most of all, the foods don't take up as much space in my "ice box" (well, sometimes I buy a small amount of ice just to keep party salads cold, allowing me to make them ahead). My favorite salads to assemble are: macaroni and olive salad, potato salad, marinated garbanzos, cucumber salad, tomato salad, carrot cole slaw, and green tossed salad. With this I usually prepare a hot rice dish, like "Nice and Spicy Rice," which can be prepared ahead then heated just before serving. The dates and nuts give a nice addition to the various flavors of the salads. I put everything in colorful bowls and plates on my galley table and ask everyone to serve themselves. It might seem like a lot of work, and perhaps it is, but it can all be done ahead of time, your table will be attractive, and you will be rewarded with very happy sailors. The leftovers can be put back in the zip-locks for tomorrow's lunch—if there are any!

Tabouli Salad

1 cup bulgur
¹/4 cup olive oil
1 cup finely chopped parsley
¹/2 cup finely chopped green onion
6 tablespoons lemon juice
¹/2 teaspoon salt
¹/8 cup fresh mint, or ¹/4 cup dried mint
1 cup chopped tomatoes

1. Pour 1 cup of boiling water over 1 cup bulgur, cover and allow to sit until water is absorbed (about 10–15 minutes). Fluff the grains with a fork.
2. Mix the prepared bulgur with the olive oil.
3. Mix the remaining ingredients with the bulgur. Chill, if possible, for several hours so the flavors blend. Garnish with cucumbers, sprouts, cherry tomatoes, and a sprinkling of sunflower seeds, as you like.

This recipe is for traditional Tabouli. It was given to me in La Paz, Baja California, at a yachtie potluck supper in 1976. I have seen many variations of Tabouli around the world, some using garlic, dill, and other herbs, but this is still my favorite.

Tomato Salad

4 tomatoes, quartered
3 small onions, sliced into rings
2 cucumbers, cut into pieces
1 cup whole kernel corn
³/4 cup yoghurt
basil or dill

Mix all of the ingredients in a large serving bowl. Chill if possible.

Bean Sprout and Rice Salad

2 cups cooked long-grain rice
2 green onions, chopped
2 carrots, thinly sliced
1 cup bean sprouts
2 bunches watercress

Dressing:
3 tablespoons lemon juice
1 teaspoon Dijon mustard
1 teaspoon sugar
4 tablespoons olive oil
2 tablespoons cream
pepper

1. Mix the dressing ingredients, then toss into the hot rice. Allow to cool.
2. Add the green onions, carrots and bean sprouts and mix well. Check the seasoning.
3. Arrange the watercress around the edge of a serving platter and spoon the salad into the center.

Tofu Dressing

1 cup tofu
3 tablespoons lemon juice
3 tablespoons oil
salt and pepper

Mash the tofu with a fork, adding the lemon juice and oil gradually to make a smooth dressing. Season to taste. You can use a blender if you have one.

Celery-Apple Salad

2 apples, chopped
4 stalks celery, chopped
$1/2$ cup nuts, broken or chopped
$1/2$ cup mayonnaise
$1/4$–$1/2$ cup apple or pineapple juice

1.   Combine apples, celery and nuts in a bowl.
2.   Mix the juice with the mayonnaise, then add to the fruit. Mix well, and serve on either a bed of lettuce leaves or shredded cabbage.

Egg Salad

4 eggs, hard boiled, roughly chopped
$1/3$ cup mayonnaise
$1/2$ teaspoon mustard
1 tablespoon pickles (sweet or dill), minced
1 tablespoon pickle juice
1 tablespoon parsley
$1/2$ teaspoon salt
dash of paprika, cayenne, and black pepper

1.   Combine the chopped eggs and pickles.
2.   Make a dressing by mixing mayonnaise, mustard, salt, pepper, cayenne, black pepper, and pickle juice.
3.   Pour dressing into egg and pickle mixture. Mix gently.
4.   Serve on lettuce as a salad, or use as a dip or sandwich spread.

I like to vary egg salad by omitting the pickles and adding chopped cucumber, chopped black olives, chopped pimento, or chopped green pepper. The addition of curry powder gives the salad a mild spicy taste, or bit of tabasco will add a bit of zing. For a milder taste, use chopped chives or dill weed.

Potato Salad

4 to 6 potatoes, unpeeled
1/3 cup vinegar
1/3 cup cooking water from potatoes
1/2 teaspoon salt
1/2 teaspoon freshly ground black pepper
1 onion, chopped
1/2 cup celery, chopped
2 or 3 hard-boiled eggs, sliced
2 to 4 tablespoons parsley, chopped
1/2 cup or more mayonnaise or 1/4 cup oil
1 teaspoon mustard

optional:
1 or 2 bell peppers, chopped
olives
carrots, chopped
dill or curry powder sprinkled on top

1. Cook the quartered potatoes. Allow to cool, then peel and slice.
2. Combine the vinegar, cooking water, and the salt and pepper, and pour over the potatoes. Gently mix in the onion, celery and other vegetables.
3. Finally, stir in the mayonnaise and mustard. Put in a bowl, garnish with sliced boiled egg and parsley, and sprinkle dill or curry powder on top.

A Quickie Salad

When conditions are difficult, you can make quite a tasty salad by opening a few cans of vegetables and mixing them in a big bowl. Add a few herbs and a dressing of your choice. Some suggestions are: green beans, beets, kidney beans, whole corn, mushrooms, lima beans, artichoke hearts—all well drained. Some herbs that blend well are basil, thyme, parsley, dill weed, and tarragon. Add a little cayenne, curry powder, chili powder, white or black pepper, or nutmeg to mayonnaise, yoghurt, oil and vinegar or lemon juice and your salad is ready to serve.

Sprouts

Sprouts are easy to grow on your boat. Sprouts (not Brussels Sprouts, but "bean" sprouts) will provide you with fresh, green, crunchy, and nutritious additions for salads, soups, and sandwiches, even while on long passages.

You can sprout almost any kind of seed, grain, or bean, but mung beans and alfalfa seeds are my favorites.

Put 1 tablespoon of mung beans in a jar and cover them with cold water. Let sit overnight. Put a cloth over the top of the jar and secure with a rubber band. Drain off the water, then lay the jar on its side in a cool dim place. Rinse the sprouts several times a day to keep them cool and moist (three to five times should do it), drain, and return to rest and grow. If you put the sprouts near sunlight you will get green shoots. Depending on the temperature and the seeds or beans, you will have shoots in three to four days. Store the sprouts in a zip-lock bag or container and keep them loose and not balled together while growing and storing.

We spent four months during the hurricane season in 1976 anchored in Conception Bay, Baja California. There were no stores close by, and to go to Mulege for shopping was an all-day hitchhiking adventure, with perhaps only five cars a day going that direction. Fresh vegetables were scarce in any case, and without refrigeration and with temperatures near 100° F, they didn't keep very well. Sprouts were our fresh-veggie main attraction. I made fresh bread every day or two, and one of our favorite lunches was hot bread, peanut butter, (maybe some mayonnaise), and sprouts. Sounds too simple, but to us it was ambrosia. And I still like it!

Basic Lemon and Oil Dressing

1/2 cup olive oil
1/3 cup water
juice of 2 lemons
salt as desired

Put the ingredients in a jar with a tight-fitting lid. Shake well to blend.

Lemon and Oil Dressing with Herbs

Add to Basic Lemon and Oil Dressing:

1/4 teaspoon basil
1/4 teaspoon oregano
1 clove garlic
2 tablespoons parsley

Make the basic dressing, shake well. Mix in the herbs and garlic.

Yoghurt Dressing

To one cup yoghurt slowly add basic lemon and oil dressing, mixing well.

Oil and Vinegar Dressing

Use 1/4 cup vinegar in place of lemon juice in basic dressing.

Tomato Dressing

Add 1/2 cup tomato puree to basic dressing, mixing well.

Soups

and

Stews

Vegetable Stew

2 tablespoons olive oil
1 large onion, chopped
4 medium carrots, chopped
4 medium potatoes, cut in cubes
2 cloves garlic, finely diced
2 stalks celery, with some of the leaves, chopped
1 red or green pepper, chopped
4 oz. TVP chunks
10 oz. can tomatoes, chopped
2 cups vegetable stock
1 tablespoon parsley
1 tablespoon tamari
freshly ground pepper

1. In a large sauce pan, heat oil and lightly brown onions.
2. Add the other chopped vegetables and sauté them for a few minutes.
3. Add the TVP chunks and brown for 3 minutes over a gentle heat.
4. Add the tomatoes and enough vegetable stock to cover the mixture. Season with the tamari and pepper. Cover and simmer for 30 to 40 minutes, or until thick and the vegetables are well cooked. Take care to add extra vegetable stock if the mixture becomes too dry.

Serve with chunks of French bread, preferably whole-wheat.

Vegetable stew is another of our favorite meals. I vary the ingredients according to what I have on hand, and what vegetables need to be used immediately. Sometimes I use chopped eggplant, which is a good replacement for mushrooms. Thyme, Herbs de Provence, oregano, and even chili powder make a good variation.

Minestrone

1 medium zucchini, sliced
1 carrot, thickly sliced and quartered
1 cup cooked garbanzos (chick-peas)
1 large stalk broccoli, cut into pieces
4 ripe tomatoes, cut into pieces
2 large onions, chopped
2 stalks celery, sliced into medium pieces
1 large green pepper, roughly chopped
³/4 cup canned corn
¹/4 pound green beans, cut into pieces
3 cloves garlic, minced
1 teaspoon basil
2 teaspoons oregano
1 tablespoon paprika
1 tablespoon oil
tamari

1. Prepare all of the vegetables, keeping them in separate piles. (Don't they look pretty?)
2. In a large sauce pan, heat the oil and sauté garlic and onions for a minute.
3. Add carrots and peppers and stir-fry a minute. Add beans, zucchini, celery, corn, broccoli, and tomatoes; stir and cook 1 to 2 minutes.
4. Add garbanzo beans and 2 quarts of boiling water. Simmer 15 to 20 minutes, adding more water if needed.
5. Add herbs and spices and simmer 4-5 minutes. Add tamari to taste.
6. Serve in large bowls with hot or toasted French bread.

I like to sprinkle grated Parmesan on top if I have it.

If you can buy Parmesan cheese in a piece (not grated) it really is tastier. It is easy to grate the cheese as you need it, using a small hand grater or a jar lid that has holes punched from the inside. The protrusions make a satisfactory grater, and you probably will always have a replacement when one gets rusty or worn out. This little hint was given to me by "Sparky" Enea, who was the cook on "Western Flyer," a commercial fishing boat from Monterey, California, used as the marine biology research vessel in John Steinbeck's Log from the Sea of Cortez.

Bean Soup

1 cup any white beans, uncooked
1 tablespoon oil
1 onion, chopped
1 carrot, diced
3 stalks celery with leaves, chopped
1 bay leaf
6-8 cups hot water
pinch of sage or marjoram (optional)
white pepper

1. Cook the beans as in basic recipe.
2. In a large sauce pan, sauté the vegetables. Add the cooked beans, hot water, and bay leaf. Simmer for about 30 minutes. Season with sage or marjoram, and white pepper.
3. If a thicker soup is desired, mash some of the mixture with a potato masher right in the pot. Serve with hot corn bread or crusty hot French bread.

To give a richness—both in flavor and nutritional value—sprinkle a tablespoon or two of yeast flakes into your soups. Stir it in during the last few minutes of cooking.

Split Pea Soup

2 cups green split peas
2 or 3 diced carrots
1 chopped onion
1 potato, diced
2 stalks celery
3 cloves garlic
¹/4 teaspoon thyme
1 tablespoon tamari
cayenne

1. Cook the peas for about 40 minutes.
2. Add the vegetables and herbs and spices and simmer another 15 minutes, until vegetables are soft.
3. Mash the peas with a potato masher. Serve hot with French or sourdough bread.

You can vary the flavor by using different herbs: sage, basil, dill or caraway seeds.

This is another soup that makes a hardy, satisfying meal on its own. In Holland, where I spent several years exploring the towns and villages by canal, I soon discovered this soup in many markets, but especially in butcher shops where the butcher prepared so many tempting foods for his delicatessen. Each had his own personal recipe, and you purchased it packaged in a plastic bag from the refrigerator. The seasoning varied from shop to shop. Other items I found were Indonesian-style fried rice, fried noodles and vegetables. After a day's travel on the canal, it was a treat to dock immediately outside a bakery, delicatessen, wine shop, or even a department store, and find a favorite dish already prepared to reheat in the galley.

Lentil Soup

2 cups lentils
2 quarts vegetable stock
1 bay leaf
2 onions, chopped
2–3 stalks celery, chopped
2 carrots, chopped
1 clove garlic, minced
tamari

1. Boil lentils in vegetable stock for 30 minutes.
2. Add the vegetables and bay leaf to the pot and simmer another 15 or 20 minutes until vegetables are soft. (Or sauté the vegetables in a small amount of oil, then add to the lentils). Season to taste with tamari.

Vegetable stock cubes can now be found in most supermarkets. You can make your own stock by boiling chopped vegetables such as green onion tops, celery tops, carrots—whatever you have—then straining the broth to get a clear liquid. We used to use the peels of these vegetables, but with such wide use of chemical fertilizers and insecticides, I don't think it is such a good idea, even if they are well scrubbed. Unfortunately, we throw away many of the nutrients with the peels.

Cornmeal Dumplings

2 oz. flour
2oz. cornmeal
1/2 teaspoon baking powder
pinch of salt
2 oz. margarine
water (enough to make stiff dough)

1. Mix all of the ingredients. Knead the dough lightly.
2. Form 8 little balls and drop into boiling water, soup or stew. Cook for 20–30 minutes.

Sandwiches,

Spreads,

and

Dips

Toppings for Burgers and Sandwiches

Select from the following:

shredded carrots
shredded cabbage
shredded radishes
sliced tomatoes
onions, red or brown, thinly sliced in rings
green onions, thinly sliced
lettuce
grated cheese
crumbled or sliced tofu
thinly sliced cucumbers
green pepper cut in thin rings
sliced beets
alfalfa sprouts

Make a dressing of the following:

yoghurt
crushed garlic
lemon juice

Make a sandwich of cooked soya burger, falafel or a tempeh patty on good, thick bread. Put the veggies on top, then spoon plenty of sauce over everything.

Alternatively, use pita, putting some of the veggies first in the bottom of the pita, then the burger and some sauce, then more veggies and more sauce.

Use any combination of the above veggies to make a hearty sandwich on French bread. Pour plenty of sauce on top. Slice in appropriate lengths. Serve with a big napkin.

Haricot Bean And Garlic Spread

4 oz. haricot beans (or any white beans)
3 tablespoons chopped fresh parsley
1 oz. butter or margarine, softened
2 cloves garlic, crushed
1/2 lemon or lime
1/4 teaspoon ground nutmeg
freshly ground pepper

1. Soak and cook beans as directed on package.
2. Mash the beans to a smooth paste. Gradually blend in the butter or margarine and parsley with the remaining ingredients. Check and adjust the seasoning and chill.

Ideal as a spread for toast or for sandwiches or as a dip with raw vegetables.

Carrot Spread

1 cup grated carrots
1 onion, grated or finely chopped
1 green pepper, finely chopped
1 teaspoon fresh ginger, finely chopped
2 tablespoons wine vinegar
mayonnaise
freshly ground pepper

1. Mix the finely chopped vegetables in a bowl.
2. Add vinegar, then stir in enough mayonnaise to make a spreadable mixture, to your taste. Season with pepper.

Serve this spread with crackers for hors d'oeuvres, or spread on bread or toast for sandwiches. It is also good for stuffing celery.

Falafel

*4 cups ground chick-peas
or chick-pea flour (garbanzo flour)
2 tablespoons curry powder
1 tablespoon paprika
¹/₂ teaspoon coriander
1 teaspoon cumin
2 tablespoons caraway seeds
1 teaspoon crushed hot red peppers
¹/₂ teaspoon each of: basil, oregano, and thyme
2 tablespoons parsley
¹/₄ cup oil
2 tablespoons tamari
2 tablespoons parsley
boiling water*

1.   Combine all of the ingredients and add enough boiling water to make a thick paste. Form into ping-pong size balls (or any shape you like). Put on a plate, and if possible refrigerate until cold. (Not necessary, but they cook more crisply when chilled).

2.   Drop 3 to 4 balls at a time into deep hot oil, and cook until well-browned all around, or fry patties in a skillet with a bit of oil. Drain well and serve. We like these served in "pita" topped with shredded carrots, onion, lettuce or shredded cabbage, and cucumber slices, with a yoghurt-garlic sauce poured on top.

Falafel are like little meatballs, but, in my opinion are much tastier. Their spicy but pleasing flavors make them popular for sandwiches as well as for appetizers. Try them with rice and tahini sauce (see "Sauces"). Falafel is popular in the Middle Eastern countries, and it is possible to buy the prepared dry mix in the United States. It is easy to make your own using this recipe. I have made the "mix" myself by combining all of the dry ingredients, storing it in a jar or zip-lock, then adding the remaining ingredients when you are ready to use it.

Eggplant Sandwiches

1 eggplant, unpeeled
2 tablespoons olive oil
basil
cheese (goat, cottage, or cream cheese)
sourdough bread
lettuce, tomatoes

1. Slice the unpeeled eggplant into thick slices (about 1 inch). Brush with oil and grill in hot skillet until tender. Sprinkle basil on the top when done. (You can broil the slices, if you prefer).
2. Toast the bread—I toast mine in a skillet on top of the stove.
3. Make sandwiches by putting on the bread: a hot slice of eggplant, some cheese, a slice of tomato, and lettuce.
4. Gently press on the sandwich to allow the juices to seep into the bread and the cheese to melt.

Eggplant is abundant in the Mediterranean countries, where this became one of our favorite sandwiches.

Another way to use eggplant in a sandwich is to place a slice of cheese on a piece of thickly sliced whole-wheat bread. Place a thin slice of onion on top of the cheese, then a slice of grilled eggplant, then a slice of tomato. Finally, top with another slice of bread. Using a heavy skillet or griddle, toast the sandwich on both sides. A slice of tofu is good in place of cheese, and since you can get "long life" tofu almost everywhere now, you can keep it on your boat without refrigeration.

Tofu Sandwich

firm tofu sliced about 1/4 inch thick
1 teaspoon olive oil, butter, or margarine
1 tablespoon tamari
tomato, sliced
onion, thinly sliced
lettuce

1. Heat oil to very hot in a heavy skillet. Add thick slices of tofu and grill until brown, turn and brown the other side.
2. Add a small amount of tamari and cook for a few seconds.
3. Place grilled tofu on thick slices of whole-wheat bread, top with onions, tomatoes, lettuce, and another piece of bread.
4. Serve hot.

Roti and Burritos

In the Caribbean "roti" are very popular and take the place of sandwiches. And in Mexico and in many parts of the United States burritos are eaten in place of sandwiches. Both of these are made in a similar way but with different ingredients. 'Roti" are large tortilla-like, thin "pancakes," filled with your choice of ingredients—usually a mild but savory mixture of curried potatoes and, perhaps, chicken, conch, fish, or vegetables. One is a complete meal. You can buy the "roti" casing in any supermarket, then concoct your own. Or, if you are ashore, any lunch spot or street vendor will surely serve "roti."

Burritos are also easy to make. Buy the tortillas in the market (either corn or flour), then fill them with refried beans, roll them into a tube, and eat plain or with salsa. You can put anything you like inside, but beans are traditional. I like a small sliver of cheese on top of the hot refried beans, with a little salsa added before they are rolled and heated on a griddle or skillet. Chopped onions are also good on top of the refried beans.

Pasta

Champignons in Yoghurt Sauce

12 oz. buckwheat noodles
2 tablespoons butter (or margarine)
1/2 pound fresh mushrooms, finely chopped
salt, pepper
1 cup low-fat plain yoghurt
1 tablespoon tamari, or soy sauce

In a large saucepan, pour boiling water over noodles. Cover and let stand 8 minutes. Drain.

Mushroom sauce:
1. In a medium skillet, melt butter. Add mushrooms. Sauté 5 minutes.
2. Season with salt and pepper. Turn off heat.
3. Stir in yoghurt and tamari.
4. Pour sauce over cooked buckwheat noodles.

Tagliatelle With Herbs and Eggs

1 pound Tagliatelle (whole-wheat if available)
2 tablespoons butter or margarine
1 bunch fresh parsley, finely chopped
1 bunch fresh basil, finely chopped
2 eggs, beaten
salt and pepper

1. Cook the noodles in salted boiling water to *al dente* (firm but tender). Drain.
2. In a large skillet, melt the butter or margarine, add parsley, basil and eggs. Season with salt and pepper.
3. Before eggs have set, add noodles. Shake the skillet so the eggs and herbs mix with the noodles.

Pasta with Green Beans

8 oz. narrow noodles
1 can French-cut green beans
(or 8 oz. fresh green beans, sliced lengthwise)
2 cloves garlic
1 tablespoon butter or margarine
oregano
freshly ground pepper
grated Parmesan
2 tablespoons tamari

1. Cook the pasta *al dente*, in salted water to prevent sogginess. Rinse with cold water and drain.
2. Steam the sliced green beans in a small amount of water until partially cooked.
3. In a large fry pan or skillet or wok, melt the butter and very lightly sauté the crushed and chopped garlic. Add the cooked green beans.
4. Mix in the drained noodles, season with tamari and a bit of freshly ground pepper, and Parmesan to taste. Serve hot or room temperature.

Linguini with Roquefort Sauce

For two persons:
1/2 pound linguini
1/4 pound Roquefort or Danish blue cheese
cream (or milk)

1. Cook the pasta as directed on the package.
2. Mash the softened cheese and mix with the cream or milk to make a thick sauce.
3. Pour the sauce over the pasta and mix gently.

One of the carrot salads or a green salad with lots of tomatoes goes well with this pasta dish.

Spinach Noodles with Vegetables

1/2 lb. spinach noodles
1 carrot, thinly sliced diagonally
1 stalk celery, sliced diagonally
1 green pepper, sliced in rings
3 green onions, thinly sliced diagonally
4 large fresh mushrooms, thinly sliced
1 small zucchini, thinly sliced
tofu, cut into cubes
2 tablespoons olive oil
few drops of sesame oil
2 tablespoons tamari
pepper

1. Cook the spinach noodles as directed on the package.
2. In a large skillet or wok, heat the olive oil and a few drops of sesame oil until very hot.
3. Add all of the vegetables and stir-fry until they are partially cooked.
4. Add the cubes of tofu and the tamari, stirring lightly for a few minutes.
5. Mix in the cooked noodles, season with pepper, and serve.

You can use any vegetables you have in this dish: use small cubes of eggplant in place of mushrooms; add a few thin slices of ginger; stir in yoghurt to make a sauce; or add wedges of tomatoes or florets of cauliflower. This makes a colorful, healthful, low calorie meal which is very easy to prepare. It can even be eaten cold.

Hot and Spicy Mexican Pasta

8 oz. package elbow macaroni
1 cup TVP
1 tablespoon olive oil
1 cup water + 1¼ oz. package taco seasoning mix
(or mix your own: cumin, garlic, chili powder, coriander, thyme)
1 large can pinto beans
1 medium-size tomato, chopped
1 cup chunky salsa
1 tablespoon chopped fresh cilantro
(or one teaspoon dried cilantro leaves)
2 oz. shredded Monterey Jack cheese with jalapeño peppers
(or Soya Kaas with jalapeño)
fresh cilantro for garnish

1. Prepare macaroni as label directs, but do not put salt in water; drain.
2. In a large skillet over high heat, brown the TVP briefly, then add the seasonings and 1 cup water; heat to boiling, stirring until blended. Reduce heat to low; simmer 5 minutes, stirring occasionally.
3. Drain pinto beans; stir into TVP mixture then add chopped tomatoes and macaroni. Heat through.
4. Mix salsa and chopped cilantro. Put the macaroni mixture onto large platter, and sprinkle with shredded cheese. Garnish with fresh cilantro. Add the seasoned salsa on top as desired.

TVP is Textured Vegetable Protein. It is made of soy, is high in protein and is an excellent meat substitute when you learn how to prepare it. You can make tasty dishes with it, and it keeps for a very long time without any special care. There are as many ways to prepare TVP as there are for hamburger, and you can flavor it with easy-to-stow ingredients like herbs, spices, peanut butter, tamari, tomato sauce, or even orange juice. TVP comes in several flavors, but I prefer to season my own, so I usually buy the plain one. You also can also get TVP in chunk style, which is excellent for making stew.

John's Spaghetti Sauce

1 onion, chopped
1 clove garlic, chopped
1 carrot, thinly sliced
1 green pepper, chopped
1 stalk celery, chopped
1 or 2 tomatoes, chopped
2 tablespoons olive oil
1 can tomato paste plus three cans of water
1/2 teaspoon each of basil, oregano, thyme
2 teaspoons fresh parsley
1/2 teaspoon freshly ground white pepper
grated Parmesan

1. Sauté all of the vegetables in the olive oil for about five or ten minutes. Add the tomato paste, plus three cans of water to the cooked vegetables, and let simmer for fifteen minutes.

2. Add the herbs and pepper during the last five minutes. (You can substitute one small can of good red wine for one of the measures of water, adding it a bit later with the herbs and pepper, letting it simmer only the last five minutes). Serve over spaghetti with Parmesan to sprinkle on the top.

You can vary the sauce by adding 1 tablespoon Parmesan to the cooked sauce. You can also add a bit of chopped eggplant sautéed with the other veggies. Or, make a mushroom sauce using only onion, garlic, spices and mushrooms (canned or fresh).

Penne Regate with Pepper Sauce

8 oz. penne regate pasta
about 8 Italian-type green peppers
(or you can use red peppers for different flavor)
1 tablespoon olive oil
water
1/4 cup cream
white pepper
Parmesan, grated

1. Cook pasta as directed on package.
2. Roughly chop the peppers. Heat the oil in a sauce pan. Add the peppers and a small amount of water (about 1/4 cup) and sauté the peppers until they are soft, adding water when necessary to keep them moist and steaming. Stir frequently.
3. When the peppers are very soft and all the water has evaporated, take off the heat. Using a blender (or a wire whisk), add the cream to the mashed peppers and mix to a smooth sauce.
4. Put the cooked penne regate in a heated serving dish and pour the pepper sauce over the top. Garnish with grated Parmesan if desired.

Although I prefer the flavor of Italian style green peppers, you can substitute Bell peppers if you peel the skins; it isn't too much trouble. Steam them for a few minutes to loosen the skin, or dunk them in boiling water for the same results. You can use them with the skins, but the sauce won't be as fine and sweet. This sauce makes a pretty dish which is both light and delicious. If you use green peppers, serve with a tossed lettuce and tomato salad with plenty of tomatoes. If you use red peppers, a cucumber salad goes well with the pasta.

Macaroni with Cheese

Many recipes for making Macaroni and Cheese tell you to boil the macaroni in plenty of water, then drain, discarding the water. Then you make a cream sauce for the thickening, adding starch to starch. Why throw out the natural thickening that comes out of the pasta? In my method, you use only enough liquid to cook the pasta, and what little is left is incorporated in the sauce. You can use milk, or part milk in cooking the macaroni, but watch it carefully as milk tends to boil over more easily.

2 cups vegetable-cooking water
(or plain water)
dash of salt
2 cups macaroni
1¹/₂ cups milk
¹/₂ cup instant powdered milk
1 cup grated cheddar-type cheese
1 tablespoon wheat germ or yeast flakes
paprika and Parmesan cheese for garnish

1. In a small sauce pan, bring water and salt to a boil.
2. Slowly sprinkle macaroni into the boiling water. Stir and continue boiling until macaroni is almost tender (about 8 minutes, or as directed on package).
3. The water should be almost absorbed; if not, stir to remove most of the moisture, then take off the heat.
4. Mix the milk with the instant powder, then stir this mixture into the macaroni.
5. Stir in the grated cheese, mixing well.
6. Sprinkle the top with wheat germ and Parmesan cheese to your taste.

You can toast the top in an oven for 15 minutes, but it is good without it.

For variations add any of the following: cooked corn, chopped green pepper, chopped onion, cooked peas, pimentos, celery or leeks. Saute the vegetables first for a different flavor, or use them freshly chopped.

Rice

and

Other

Grains

Rice

I have seen so many varieties of rice around the world: brown and white, long grain, short grain, broken grain, even medium grain. In general, the short grain rice cooks softer and a little bit "gooier." The long grain is drier, and therefore better for dishes like fried rice and Mexican rice. Brown rice often takes longer to cook, but in all cases you have to experiment and learn what you like best. From one brand to another, and from one country to another, the cooking times will vary, as will the amount of water needed. I was taught the following basic method of cooking rice by a woman in Japan:

1 cup rice
1 1/2 cups cold water
(2 cups water for brown rice)

1.   Wash and drain well one cup of rice.
2.   Put it in a sauce pan and add 1 1/2 cups of water and a pinch of salt. Bring to a boil, stir only once, and put a tight-fitting lid on the pot.
3.   Cook on *very* low heat for 15 minutes (20–45 minutes for brown rice, or until all water is absorbed). No peeking!
4.   Turn off the heat and let stand *at least* 15 minutes before serving.
5.   Very gently fork through the rice from the bottom to let the steam rise through the rice and make it fluffy.

If you are going to let it sit longer than 15 minutes, wrap the pot in a towel to keep it warm.

Here's another way to measure the amount of cooking water: level the uncooked rice in the bottom of the pan, then add enough water to come to the first joint of your index finger. It works regardless of the size of the pot or the quantity of rice!

Fried Rice

4 cups cooked brown rice
1 onion, finely chopped
1/2 green pepper, finely chopped
1 small carrot, finely diced
1 small stalk celery, finely diced
2 eggs, scrambled
1/3 cup peas
2 tablespoons oil
2 tablespoons tamari or soy sauce
pepper

1. In a wok or skillet, fry the onion in the oil until starting to brown. Add the rest of the raw vegetables, stir-frying until they are beginning to soften. Add the cold, cooked rice and toss until the rice is hot throughout.

2. Add a little more oil if necessary. Add the peas. Stir the scrambled eggs into the fried rice, add the tamari or soy sauce and mix well. Pepper lightly. Sprigs of parsley on top make a pretty dish!

If you have a wok, you can push the rice mixture aside, break the eggs in the bottom of the wok and scramble them there, mixing them into the rice after they are set.

Cardamom Rice

2 tablespoons butter or margarine
1 tablespoon oil
1 small onion, chopped
1 clove garlic, crushed
l cup long-grain rice
1 teaspoon curry powder
1/4 teaspoon ground cumin
1 1/2 cups vegetable stock or water
2 tablespoons lemon juice
1 bay leaf
3 cardamom pods, crushed
8 oz. raisins
1 tablespoon blanched almonds, halved
2 tablespoons unsalted peanuts
1 tablespoon cashew nuts
salt and pepper to taste
coriander leaves or parsley to garnish

1. Sauté onions in butter and oil 3 minutes.
2. Add rice and fry, stirring occasionally, until opaque.
3. Add curry powder, cinnamon and cumin, fry for 1/2 minute, then add stock or water, bay leaf, cardamom, raisins, salt and pepper. Bring to boil, cover and simmer for 15 minutes.
4. Spread nuts in a pan, toast until golden.
5. Remove the bay leaf from the cooked rice, stir in nuts. Garnish with fresh parsley or coriander. Serve hot.

Mexican Rice

1 cup rice
2 tablespoons oil
1 onion, chopped
1 clove garlic, chopped
1 green pepper, chopped
1 stalk celery, diced
2 teaspoons chili powder
1/2 teaspoon cumin seeds
few drops of lemon juice
1 can whole peeled tomatoes
1 cup water

1. Heat oil in a large heavy skillet, add rice and stir-fry until the rice begins to brown slightly.

2. Add onions and garlic and continue cooking for a minute. Add chili powder and cumin seeds, stirring through the rice mixture, cooking another minute.

3. Add the rest of the raw vegetables and cook a few minutes more.

4. Take the pan off the heat for a few minutes, then add a few drops of lemon juice and the can of tomatoes (slightly chopped in the can) and the juice. Place back on the heat for a few minutes, then stir in a cup of water. (The liquid from the tomatoes plus the water should be about 1 1/2 to 2 cups).

5. Cover and cook for about 15–20 minutes, or until the rice is done, mixing lightly a few times while cooking.

6. Cook for a few minutes more with the lid off, mixing from the bottom of the pan with a spatula. Let sit covered for 15 minutes before serving. The rice grains should be separated and the entire mixture on the dry side rather than mushy.

Note: Carrots and corn can be added, sautéeing the carrots with the other vegetables, and adding the corn towards the end of the cooking period. This makes a good vegetable-rice casserole, and when served with a green salad you have a complete meal.

Grenadian Rice and Peas

1 cup long-grain rice, washed and drained
1 cup coconut milk
1 cup water
1 small onion, chopped
1 small green pepper, diced
1 teaspoon chopped fresh ginger
1 carrot, diced
1/8 teaspoon celery seeds
1 cup cooked pigeon peas, black-eyed peas, or chick-peas
1 tablespoon tamari (or soy sauce)
pepper

1. Put all of the ingredients except the cooked peas in a pot with a tight-fitting lid. (Or, you can use your pressure cooker).
2. Simmer slowly for 15 minutes, when the liquid should be almost absorbed. Add the peas, and let cook on very low heat for another 5 minutes.
3. Turn off the heat and let sit covered for about 10 minutes.
4. Serve with cole slaw or other green salads.

You can use canned coconut milk if you can't make your own, but be sure it doesn't have sugar added to it.

There are many variations of this dish, sometimes called Rice Cook-Up in Grenada: you can add a clove of garlic, 1 carrot, a stalk of diced celery, and a small amount of hot pepper sauce found all around the Caribbean. You can also sauté the veggies in a small amount of oil before adding them to the rice to cook. This makes a savory, hearty and easy lunch dish.

Indian Rice With Red Peppers and Papaya

1 cup long-grain rice
2 cups water
1¹/₂–2¹/₄ cups sliced and diced red pepper
¹/₄ cup pecan pieces (or other nuts)
2 tablespoons chopped fresh parsley
3 large scallions, chopped
1–2 tablespoons olive oil
3 tablespoons red wine vinegar
¹/₂ teaspoon minced garlic
1 teaspoon ground cumin
1 teaspoon ground coriander (or oregano)
¹/₄ cup raisins
1 ripe papaya
black pepper to taste
(fresh ginger is a good addition)

1. Combine rice with water. Heat to boil, reduce heat and simmer with tight-fitting lid for 17 minutes, or until water is absorbed.
2. Toast nuts until lightly browned.
3. In serving bowl combine oil, vinegar, garlic, scallions, red peppers and spices.
4. Stir in cooked rice.
5. Cut papaya into large cubes and add to mixture.

This recipe was given to me by Karen on the s/v "Flow" while we were anchored in Hog Island, Grenada, West Indies. She and Horst spent several months anchored next to me. ("Flow" is Horst's last name spelled backwards!) Karen is from California, and Horst, from Salzburg, Austria, is a pianist and has a professional keyboard on his boat. We had many musicians in the anchorage and an assortment of instruments, including 2 flutes, several recorders, guitar, keyboards, violin, and a harmonica. Although Karen is not a vegetarian, she prepared wonderfully delicious vegetarian food for me, which was enjoyed by all during our musical evenings aboard "Flow."

Arroz Verde

2 tablespoons oil
2 green peppers, cored, seeded and chopped
1 large chili, seeded and chopped
3 green onions, chopped
1 clove garlic, crushed
6 tablespoons chopped parsley
8 oz. long-grain rice
2 cups vegetable stock or water
pepper
2 hard-boiled eggs, quartered, to garnish

1.   Heat oil in a large pan; add peppers, chili, green onions and garlic and fry until softened.

2.   Add the remaining ingredients, bring to boil, cover and simmer for 15 minutes or until the rice is tender.

3.   Fork the rice through and pile into a warmed serving dish. Arrange the eggs on top to serve.

If you have leftover rice from most any of these rice dishes, you can press it into a lightly buttered or oiled square plastic container or a cake pan, slice it into large squares, then fry it in a hot skillet until lightly browned. Serve with a brown miso or mushroom gravy or sauce.

Kitchedi

1/2 lb. red lentils
1 1/4 lb. long-grain rice
6 cups boiling water
3 tablespoons butter or ghee
2 large brown onions, chopped
3 cloves garlic, crushed
1-inch piece fresh ginger, finely chopped
1/8 teaspoon turmeric
3 pods cardamom, broken in mortar
2-inch stick cinnamon bark
4 cloves
a few whole peppercorns
2 hard-boiled eggs
chopped green onions, mint or parsley

1. Wash and soak lentils in water for 1 hour. Drain.
2. Tie cinnamon, cloves, cardamom, and peppercorns in a piece of gauze.
3. Wash rice in a sieve and let drain.
4. Heat butter (or preferably, ghee) in a heavy pot. Sauté onions, ginger, garlic, and turmeric until soft.
5. Stir in the drained rice, and fry it until it becomes yellowish and transparent, stirring constantly.
6. Add about 6 cups boiling water and boil without a lid for about 5–10 minutes, then add drained lentils and bag of spices.
7. Continue boiling, and when the water is just disappearing from the surface, remove pan from stove, cover with a tight-fitting lid, wrap everything in two large bath towels, and let it cook in its own steam for an hour or so.
8. To serve, remove the bag of spices, spoon mixture into a large bowl, and garnish with slices of egg and chopped green onions.

Be sure to remove the spice bag! An Australian doctor in New Guinea helped himself to an "extra treat" from the pot one evening, and felt a bit worse for wear the following day.

Kitchedi is an excellent meal in itself, and especially good and nourishing for a hungry crew. It is also an excellent dish to take to a potluck dinner because it will stay hot for a long while (wrapped in towels). This recipe comes from an Indian couple I met in the canals of France who were sailing their second yacht from England to India. The first, unfortunately, was lost on a reef in the Red Sea, about which he wrote a book.

Mild Curry Spice Pilaf

2 tablespoons oil
1 onion, chopped
1 cup long-grain rice
1 teaspoon turmeric
1/2 teaspoon ground coriander
pinch of ground cloves
1 1/2-2 cups vegetable stock or water
lemon slices and parsley to garnish

1. Heat the oil in a large skillet, add the onion and sauté until softened. Add the rice and fry for about 2 minutes, until it turns opaque.

2. Sprinkle in the spices and fry for about 1 minute. Pour in the stock or water, add the bay leaf, salt, and pepper.

3. Bring to boil, cover, turn the heat down to low, and simmer for 15 minutes or until the rice is tender. Garnish with lemon and parsley to serve.

Nice and Spicy Rice

1 tablespoon oil
1 onion, chopped
1/2 carrot, finely chopped
1 clove garlic, finely chopped
1/2-inch piece fresh ginger, finely chopped
1 cup long-grain rice
1 1/2 cups hot water
1-inch piece cinnamon
1/4 teaspoon ground cloves
1/4 teaspoon freshly ground nutmeg
1 teaspoon curry powder
2 cardamom pods, broken open
dash celery seeds
2 tablespoons tamari
2 tablespoons peanuts, freshly roasted
2 tablespoons date bits

1. In a large heavy skillet, heat the oil. Add chopped onion, carrot, garlic and ginger. Stir-fry for a couple of minutes.
2. Add the spices and continue to stir-fry a few more minutes.
3. Add the well-washed and drained rice. Cook another few minutes, stirring to coat the rice with the spices.
4. Carefully add the hot water. Mix well. Bring to a boil, then turn heat down to very low. Put a tight-fitting lid on the pot and let simmer at very low heat for 15 minutes.
5. Turn off the heat, and let the rice sit for another 15 minutes or more. It's a good idea to cover the pot with a heavy towel.
6. After sitting, stir through rice with a fork, allowing steam to pass throughout and separate the rice. At this time, stir in the peanuts and dates. Season with tamari.

This is one of my favorite dishes to prepare to take to the beach or to another boat for potluck. It keeps well and is even good the next day (perhaps even better).

Miso Rice

1. Cook rice as you would in basic recipe.
2. For every cup of uncooked rice you will need 2 rounded tablespoons of miso.
3. Soften miso in a little warm water.
4. When rice has cooked and all the water is dissolved, stir in miso, cover again and immediately remove from heat.
5. Allow to sit 10 minutes before serving.
6. Fork through to separate grains, and serve warm.

"Miso" is a fermented soy product which you can find in most health food stores or in the specialty section of some supermarkets. It is made from soy beans, water and sea salt and aged in a barrel for two to three years. Hacho miso is the strongest; mugi is a medium-strength miso containing barley; and komo miso is the lightest, aged two years and is made with brown rice in addition to the soy beans, water and sea salt. They are all a dark brown paste, keep well, and impart a richness to soups, vegetables, gravies, and stews.

Rice Balls

Have you ever had rice balls? In Hawaii they are very popular for picnics, and they keep well without refrigeration for a day. To make them, boil rice until it is soft but not mushy. Then, without letting it steam in the pan, quickly spread it out in a large cake pan or plate. Immediately sprinkle the top with a light Japanese-style vinegar and let sit until cool. With lightly buttered or oiled hands, form large orange-sized balls, packing the rice grains firmly together. You can put a small piece of fruit or vegetable in the center of the ball if you like. Traditionally, the balls are wrapped in seaweed soaked in a little tamari or soy sauce, but if you don't have this, they are still good just plain.

Pulses

Mexican Beans

2 cups pinto beans (soaked overnight)
2 tablespoons olive oil
1 large brown onion
2 cloves garlic, chopped
1 teaspoon cumin seeds
3 tablespoons chili powder
1/2 teaspoon coriander
1 green pepper, chopped
1 or 2 stalks celery, chopped
1 large can whole peeled tomatoes, chopped in can
(1/2 cup TVP soya granules, optional)

1. Cook the beans in a pressure cooker for 40 minutes, or boil in enough water to cover for 1 1/2 hours or until soft.

2. In a separate pan, sauté the onions and garlic in 2 tablespoons of olive oil until soft. Add the cumin seeds, cook for a minute, then add the chili powder and cook another minute, stirring the spices into the onions and garlic. Add the remaining chopped fresh veggies and the optional soya granules and sauté for about five minutes.

3. Finally, add the can of chopped tomatoes and 1/2 teaspoon coriander. Simmer for another five minutes.

4. Add this mixture to the cooked beans. Let everything simmer for at least fifteen minutes.

5. Serve in large bowls with side dishes of chopped onion and grated cheddar cheese to sprinkle on top. Corn bread and a salad completes the meal.

Mexican beans are excellent served on rice with grated cheese, finely chopped onions and green peppers sprinkled on top. A bowl of hot sauce can be served on the side for those who like it extra hot, and a bowl of plain yoghurt for those who like a milder taste. Goat cheese goes great with Mexican dishes.

We also like the variation of serving these Mexican beans with macaroni, which we call Chili-Mac. Don't forget the cornbread!

Butter Beans with Herbs

6 oz. package soft cream cheese
6 tablespoons milk
2 cups butter beans already cooked
2 tablespoons chopped parsley
3 sprigs chopped thyme
2 tablespoons chopped chives
salt and pepper
thyme leaves for garnish

1.   Place the cheese and milk in a pan and warm gently, stirring until melted and smooth.
2.   Add the beans, stirring gently to coat with the cheese sauce.
3.   Stir in the herbs and season with salt and pepper. Serve immediately, garnished with fresh thyme.

You can used herbed cream cheese in place of the plain style, omitting the additional herbs. This is a very simple yet tasty dish.

Garbanzos with Tahini Sauce

2 cups garbanzo beans (chick-peas)
¹/₄ cup tahini
2 tablespoons tamari

1.   Cook beans as usual. Garbanzos may take a little longer than other beans.
2.   When almost cooked, stir in the tahini and tamari and cook for another 30 minutes over low heat. If you have used a pressure cooker, open it and stir in the ingredients after about 40 minutes, then simmer without the lid for another 15-20 minutes.

The tahini will make a nice gravy. If you like, you can add onions, garlic, mushrooms or tomatoes. I like it as it is with just the tahini and tamari.

Catalan Alubias with Aselgas

*1 cup dried alubias (or any other white beans like
navy beans, haricots, or garbanzos)*

1. Soak the beans in water overnight.
2. Drain, add a bay leaf and sufficient water for cooking.
3. Cook in pressure cooker about 30–45 minutes, or in a normal pot for 1 1/2 hours or until soft.

*1 1/2 pounds aselgas, Swiss chard, or spinach, roughly cut
1 or 2 cloves garlic, finely chopped
1/2 cup raisins
1 or 2 tablespoons pine nuts or slivered almonds
white pepper*

1. Sauté the chopped garlic in a large pot or skillet until soft.
2. Wash the greens, and put them in the pot along with the water that clings to them. Steam with lid on, stirring occasionally, until the greens are soft.
3. Add the alubias and other ingredients and cook a bit more until all the flavors are well blended.
4. Serve in a large soup plate or dish.

This is very good with garlic bread made with a little oregano sprinkled on top of the bread.

The above is the Catalan version. In the south of Spain this dish is made with potatoes and onions in place of the beans, omitting the raisins and piñones. Good too.

Lentil Stir-Fry

3/4 cup lentils
2 tablespoons oil
1 onion, chopped
1 green pepper, chopped
2 cloves garlic, smashed and chopped
1 stalk celery, sliced
1 or 2 tomatoes, peeled and chopped
1/2 teaspoon cumin seeds
1 teaspoon chili powder

1. Soak lentils in water to cover for 30 minutes. Cook until tender, about 20 minutes.
2. Sauté the onions in oil until soft, add the cumin seeds and cook another minute. Then add the chili powder and cook another minute.
3. Add the rest of the vegetables and stir-fry until soft.
4. Add the lentils and cook until heated through and flavors blend. Salt as desired.

Lentil Egg Curry

4 eggs, hard-boiled
3/4 cup lentils
2 brown onions, sliced
2–3 tablespoons ghee or butter
1 tablespoon Indian curry powder

1. Soak lentils in water overnight.
2. Fry sliced onions in a saucepan until golden.
3. Add curry powder, mix well, then add lentils.
4. Cook for 5 minutes, stirring constantly.
5. Add 1/2 cup hot water, and simmer until the lentils are tender and all the water has been absorbed.
6. Cut the hard-boiled eggs into halves and add to the lentils just before serving.

Lima Beans with Fennel Seeds

1 tablespoon olive oil
¹/₂ tablespoon fennel seeds
1 clove garlic, finely chopped
1 cup diced celery
1¹/₂ cups diced red sweet pepper
small bunch spinach leaves, washed and trimmed
(about 2 cups lightly packed)
3¹/₃ cups firm-cooked lima beans
salt and freshly ground black pepper to taste

1. Heat half of the oil in a large skillet over medium-low heat. Add fennel seeds and garlic and cook until seeds darken slightly. Stir in celery and peppers and cook just until soft, about 4 to 5 minutes.

2. Stack spinach leaves, roll into a tight cigar-shape and cut crosswise into fine shreds. Add shredded spinach and beans to the skillet and cook just until the beans are warm and the spinach is wilted. Season with salt and generous grindings of pepper, then drizzle with remaining oil. Serves 6.

I have found lentils in almost every country that I have visited around the world. They come in many colors, and all are easier to cook than beans, which usually require overnight soaking or a long cooking time. Lentils which have been soaked about 30 minutes require only 20 to 30 minutes boiling, or about 10 minutes in a pressure cooker—less time than it takes to boil pasta or rice. My favorite is the red one, which is the fastest cooking, but all of them are quite nutritious, easy to cook, and good to eat. All legumes will cook faster if salt or oil is <u>not</u> added during cooking. Since lentils keep so well, are fast cooking, and are a good source of protein, they make an excellent replacement for meat. You can make patties from cooked lentils which rival any hamburger. Seasoned lentils and vegetables on rice or macaroni is an easy meal to prepare, and a very satisfying one.

Lentil Loaf

8 oz. red lentils
1 bay leaf
2 tablespoons olive oil
1 large or 2 medium onions, finely chopped
clove garlic, finely chopped
3/4 cup bread crumbs
4–6 oz. cheese, grated
1 egg, beaten
1/2 cup vegetable stock
1/2 cup minced parsley
1/2 teaspoon thyme
1 tablespoon tamari
dash each pepper and nutmeg

1. Soak the lentils 30 minutes, then cook in 2 cups of water for 25 minutes, when all water will have been absorbed.

2. Fry the onions and garlic in olive oil until well browned. Mix the cooked lentils with the fried onions and garlic, then add the rest of the ingredients. Turn the mixture into a well-greased loaf pan.

3. Bake at 375°F for 35 to 40 minutes.

4. Serve hot with miso mushroom gravy and vegetables, or use cold slices in sandwiches.

This is one of my favorites. It is a good dish to take to potluck beach parties and everybody likes it.
Try using the above mixture in a pizza or pie shell. Sprinkle some grated cheese on top before cooking, or spoon yoghurt on top after cooking.

Potato and Lentil Patties

1 cup lentils
1 bay leaf
2 oz. grated cheese
1 egg, beaten
1 teaspoon yeast extract (Marmite)
1 tablespoon hot water
2 cups mashed potatoes
1 cup bread crumbs
1 cup onions, finely chopped
mixed herbs to your taste
(thyme, sage, garlic powder, etc.)
salt and pepper
2-4 tablespoons oil

1. Soak lentils in water to cover (about 2 cups) for 20 minutes.
2. Add bay leaf and simmer lentils for about 20 minutes, until water is absorbed.
3. Sauté onions in a small amount of oil.
4. Dissolve yeast extract in hot water and add to cooked lentils.
5. Add beaten egg, grated cheese, mashed potatoes, sautéed onions, seasonings, and half of the bread crumbs, or sufficient to make a mixture stiff enough to form rissoles or thick patties. Roll rissoles or cover patties with bread crumbs.
6. Heat the oil in a hot skillet, then fry patties until brown on both sides.

Serve hot with vegetables and your favorite gravy (miso gravy, mushroom, etc.).

Vegetable Main Dishes

Altea Attraction

1 can artichoke hearts
4 tablespoons olive oil
1 onion, sliced in rings
1 red pepper, sliced in rings
1 green pepper, sliced in rings
4 tablespoons flour
2 cups milk
1 tablespoon tamari
1/2 teaspoon sage leaves
white pepper

1.   Drain the can of artichoke hearts, then douse them with a few spoons of olive oil. Let sit for 1/2 hour.

2.   In a frying pan, sauté the onion and pepper slices in a small amount of olive oil. When soft add the artichoke hearts and cook until brownish.

3.   Remove from the frying pan to a casserole. In the same frying pan, make a roux of 4 tablespoons of whole-wheat flour in about as much oil, then slowly add 2 cups of milk, stirring with a whisk. Cook very slowly until the sauce is thickened (adjusting if necessary with more milk).

4.   Add 1 tablespoon tamari, sage, and pepper. Pour over veggies and serve over green noodles (or rice, or boiled potatoes). This is also good with Lentil Loaf.

August 27 is John's birthday. As usually seems to be the case on his birthday, we were at anchor—this particular year in Altea, a harbor on the Mediterranean coast of Spain. After an early dinner of the above concoction, we set sail for the island of Ibiza in the Balearic Islands off the coast of Spain. A spectacular sunset followed the receding thunderstorms, then the twinkling lights along the coast to Cabo de Nao entertained us until about midnight. We could see the light from Nao Lighthouse for several hours. It was a good passage, the morning was sparkling after a hazy night, and our landfall exciting to watch from on the horizon.

Cauliflower and Fennel Pie

2 recipes Whole-wheat Pastry
1 small cauliflower, broken in florets
2 heads fresh fennel, trimmed and quartered
1 large onion, cut in chunks
2 tablespoons butter or margarine
4 tablespoons all-purpose flour
1³/4 cups vegetable stock
2 tablespoons soy sauce
1 tablespoon Dijon-style mustard
freshly ground black pepper

1. If using an oven, preheat it to 400°F. Grease a 3-inch deep casserole.
2. Make a pastry as directed in the following recipe. Line the prepared pie dish with 2/3 of the pastry.
3. In a large sauce pan, boil florets, fennel and onion in a small amount of water 5 minutes or until tender. Drain, saving water for stock.
4. Arrange vegetables in pastry shell, packing tightly.
5. In a medium sauce pan, melt butter or margarine. Stir in flour to make a roux.
6. In a small bowl, mix vegetable stock, soy sauce and mustard. Add liquid mixture slowly to roux. Season with pepper. Pour sauce over vegetables in pastry shell.
7. On a lightly floured surface, roll out remaining pastry. Cover pie with pastry, pressing edges together firmly.
8. Grease a piece of waxed paper. Cover top of pie with the waxed paper. Bake in preheated oven 40 minutes. Remove waxed paper after 30 minutes. Serve hot.

Whole-wheat Pastry

1 cup whole-wheat flour
1/2 teaspoon baking powder
1/2 teaspoon salt
1/4 cup butter or margarine
2 tablespoons corn oil
2 to 3 tablespoons water

1. In a medium bowl, mix flour, baking powder and salt.
2. Using a pastry blender or 2 knives, cut in butter or margarine until mixture resembles coarse crumbs. Slowly stir in oil and water, making a stiff paste.
3. Wrap in plastic wrap or waxed paper. Refrigerate 1 hour if possible.
4. Remove pastry from refrigerator. Let stand until pastry is at room temperature before rolling out.

Use for Cauliflower and Fennel Pie or for any vegetable pie.

This is a very nice pastry, and it bakes quite well in a Dutch oven. Sometimes I like to bake it just a little before filling with a vegetable and sauce mixture.

Vegetable Curry

1 large onion, chopped
2 cloves garlic, chopped
1/2-inch piece of ginger root, thinly sliced
2 tablespoons olive oil
1/2 teaspoon each of cumin seeds, mustard seeds, fenugreek seeds
3 teaspoons curry powder
1/2 teaspoon hot chili powder
2 carrots, roughly sliced
1 potato cut into large cubes
1 small eggplant, unpeeled, cubed
1 green pepper, chopped
1 to 3 tomatoes, chopped
1 stalk celery, chopped
1 can of whole peeled tomatoes (chopped in the can)
water or vegetable water

1. In a large skillet lightly sauté the onion, garlic and ginger in olive oil.
2. Push veggies to the sides of the pan, add the cumin seeds and cook for a half minute, then add the other seeds and cook until the seeds begin to pop.
3. Add the curry and chili powder. Cook for a few seconds. Add the remaining veggies, mix well and cook a few seconds more.
4. Add enough liquid to cover. Simmer for about 20 minutes, or until the veggies are cooked.
5. Serve on rice or cous cous.
   (Soya chunks or granules can be added with the spices, if desired).

I learned to make curry when we were in Fiji in 1979. The public market in Suva was huge, and you could find almost any type of fruit and vegetable there. But to me, the most exciting area was the herb and spice section—the aromas were tantalizing! Each vendor, usually Indian, had very large wooden boxes and bins containing spices from all around the world. I easily imagined the sailing ships of earlier days, arriving in Suva Harbor just as we had, but unloading crates and bags of spices. And, the variety of curries we found in the islands was unending: each person I talked with had their own version of how to make curry. The above recipe is a very simple one which I put in this book for John. However, the variations are endless, and I don't think I ever make it the same way twice. Don't be shy to use whatever vegetables you have on hand, and vary the spices to your taste or their availability. Unless you have a favorite "curry powder," it is much better to make your own by grinding the fresh spices in a mortar. When I make curry, the whole dock knows it from the aroma wafting in the air.

Cous Cous

1 cup cous cous
1¹/₂ cups water or vegetable water

Put the cous cous in a bowl and sprinkle the boiling water over the top of them, mixing well. Put a cover on the bowl and allow the cous cous to steam and soak up the water (about 15 minutes). Using a fork, fluff the grains.

If desired, melt a tablespoon of butter or margarine in a skillet, add the cous cous and stir-fry for a few seconds.

Serve with Vegetable Curry.

To serve: Put the cous cous on individual serving plates. Put the curried vegetables with plenty of juice on the cous cous, then top with plain yoghurt.

High Water Gibraltar

2 large potatoes, thickly sliced
2 carrots, thinly sliced diagonally
1 large onion, sliced in thick rings
1 small eggplant, sliced in 1/2-inch pieces
1 or 2 small zucchini, sliced
2 cloves garlic, crushed
1 large tomato, sliced
1/2 teaspoon basil
2 tablespoons oil
Parmesan
<u>Sauce</u>
2 tablespoons margarine, butter, or oil
2 tablespoons whole-wheat flour
1 cup milk
1 cup cooking water from the potatoes
1 tablespoon tamari or soy sauce

1. Boil the potato and carrot slices in a small amount of water until partially cooked. Save the cooking water.

2. In a large frying pan or casserole, sauté onion rings in oil. Add (layering) eggplant, zucchini, and the partially cooked potatoes and carrots. Add pressed garlic over the top, gently stirring it through the mixture. Lastly, place tomato slices on top of everything.

3. In a small sauce pan make a roux of the flour and oil, then slowly add the milk and potato water, stirring with a whisk until smooth. Season with tamari, and cook until sauce begins to thicken, making a medium thick sauce.

4. Pour the sauce over the veggies, letting it mix into them. Cook over low heat or bake for about 20 minutes.

5. Sprinkle Parmesan cheese over the top during the last 5 minutes. Sprinkle basil over the top and serve.

We started naming some of my concoctions in honor of the place we happened to be when it was created. Usually they were made from whatever I had on hand, and cooked however I was able under the circumstances. Altea Attraction, Maupiti Melange, and High Water Gibraltar are a few examples, and often they would be noted in the log book if we especially liked them.

We were in Gibraltar for three weeks waiting for favorable weather and tides to leave the Mediterranean on our way to Puerto Sherry on the Atlantic coast of Spain. "Playing" the tidal streams rushing through the Strait is essential for a small boat, hence our preoccupation with the tide tables. After a lengthy wait, we finally synchronized an easterly wind with an early morning ebb stream. We had a fast and exhilarating sail around Tarifa to Barbate, where we anchored and then were weather-bound for another week (but in a much cleaner and relaxing setting).

Lima Bean Pot

2 cups lima beans
2 carrots, sliced
1 onion, chopped
2 cloves garlic, crushed and chopped
1/2 green pepper, chopped
1 stalk chopped celery
1 tablespoon olive oil
1 small can tomato sauce
1 tablespoon brown sugar
1 teaspoon chili powder
1/8 teaspoon cayenne
1 teaspoon salt

1. Cook lima beans by your usual method.
2. Sauté vegetables in oil until soft. Add the remaining ingredients, stir and cook a few minutes.
3. Add the vegetable sauce to the beans and cook for 20 minutes.

We like thick, hot cornbread to go with Lima Bean Pot.

Stir-Fried Veggies

Various vegetables, thinly sliced:
Carrots, green onions, green pepper, celery,
green beans, eggplant, ginger root, garlic,
green leaf cabbage or bok choy, zucchini,
tomato wedges, whatever you may have
Tofu, cut in cubes
2 tablespoons oil
2 tablespoons tamari
pepper

In a wok or large skillet heat the oil to very hot. Add the veggies one type at a time, starting with the onions, sliced ginger, and garlic. Then add the slower cooking veggies followed by the faster cooking ones. Stir after each addition. Add the tofu cubes last. Put a lid on the pan to lightly steam the veggies, adding a couple tablespoons of water if necessary to produce steam. When everything is cooked to your liking, add the tamari and stir lightly. Pepper to taste. Serve over rice or stir into cooked noodles or spaghetti. Spinach noodles are especially good.

Vegetable Rice Stir-Up

1 cup brown rice
2 cups water
3/4 cup TVP granules (mince)
2 cloves garlic, chopped
4 thin slices fresh ginger
3/4 cup boiling water (to just cover)
1 tablespoon peanut butter
2 eggs
2 tablespoons oil
1 cup cooked mixed vegetables
1 tablespoon tamari
Salt and pepper to taste
1 tablespoon fresh parsley, chopped
Freshly grated nutmeg

1. Cook brown rice as usual in covered pan for 30 minutes or until all water is absorbed. Let stand covered about 15 minutes.

2. Soak TVP in hot water with chopped garlic, ginger, and peanut butter for about 15 minutes.

3. Heat oil in a wok or large skillet, add TVP mixture and stir-fry about 5 minutes.

4. Add cooked rice and mixed vegetables, mix, and cook another five minutes.

5. Push rice mixture to the sides of the pan, pour 1 teaspoon of oil into center and break eggs into the hot oil.

6. Scramble eggs until set, then stir into rice mixture. Lower heat.

7. Stir in tamari and pepper to taste. Add parsley and freshly grated nutmeg.

This dish can be prepared with almost any leftover vegetables you might have: peas, carrots, green beans, chopped broccoli, corn, black-eyed peas, and sliced Brussel sprouts are but a few suggestions. Chopped nuts also add cruchiness and good flavor, or grated cheese will add a creamy texture. The dish is even tastier after sitting, allowing the flavors to blend.

Eggplant Parmesan

2 medium-large eggplant
2 cups grated mozzarella cheese
2 cups seasoned tomato sauce (oregano, basil,
onion, garlic, etc.)
2 eggs, beaten
1 cup seasoned bread crumbs
1/4 to 1/2 cup olive oil

1. Slice eggplant in rounds 1/2-inch thick. Salt both sides and allow to stand 1/2 hour. Rinse well and pat dry with paper towel.
2. Heat approximately 2 tablespoons of olive oil in large fry pan or griddle.
3. Dip eggplant in egg, bread crumbs, and then egg again.
4. Fry eggplant in oil approximately 10 minutes each side, or until moderately soft. Add small quantities of oil as necessary.
5. Layer in casserole dish: 1/2 cup tomato sauce, layer of eggplant, grated cheese. Repeat layers and finish with tomato sauce and light layer of cheese.
6. Bake in 350° oven 30 minutes or until bubbling. Allow to stand 5 or 10 minutes before serving.

This is a delicious dish, and although it is best cooked in a real oven, you can improvise with a Dutch oven. This is another great recipe from Karen and Horst of the Austrian sailing yacht "Flow," whom I met in Hog Island, on the south coast of Grenada in the West Indies. After dinner we had a musical treat with Ian of the English catamaran "Manx Cat" playing flute and Wolfgang on the German sailing yacht "Al Capo" playing guitar. Karen is a great cook, and although not a vegetarian, she always served excellent vegetarian dinners when I was dining aboard. Everybody else enjoyed the change, too.

Biksemad is a family dish I learned to make in Denmark. It is a variation of American hashed browns and something like the southern version of hash my mother used to make on Mondays with Sunday's leftovers. Biksemad means "bride's food" in Danish, probably because you really can't go wrong making it. The following is my vegetarian version.

Biksemad

2 large potatoes, thinly sliced or chopped
1 large onion, chopped
1 carrot, chopped
1 green pepper, chopped
2 or 3 tablespoons olive oil
salt and pepper

1. Heat a large, heavy skillet that has a good lid. Add olive oil.
2. When the oil is hot, add potatoes and other vegetables. Stir to coat everything with the oil. Fry for a few minutes to brown the potatoes, then cover and let steam, turning frequently as the bottom portions brown. After potatoes begin to soften, leave the lid off and continue cooking until everything is done.
3. Salt and pepper to taste.

We like to put either Mexican salsa or Caribbean hot sauce on Biksemad. Probably not very Danish, though.

Huevos Rancheros

2 tomatoes, chopped fine
1 green pepper, chopped
1 onion, chopped
1–2 teaspoons chili powder
4 tablespoons tomato sauce
Tabasco sauce
4 eggs
tortillas, beans, or rice

1. Sauté the vegetables until soft. Add chili powder when they are partially cooked, and mix thoroughly.

2. Add tomato sauce. Simmer for 5 minutes.

3. Carefully break the eggs on top of the sauce (make a little nest for each of them), spacing them evenly. Continue to simmer gently, spooning some of the mixture over the eggs as they begin to set.

4. Serve over warm tortillas—the traditional way—or refried or mashed pinto or red beans, or rice.

Huevos Rancheros makes a very hearty breakfast or a satisfying supper. Have a stack of warm tortillas wrapped in a cloth on the table, along with butter or margarine. Hold the tortilla in the palm of your hand, spread a thin layer of butter on the tortilla, then roll it to a cigar shape to eat. Watch that the melting butter doesn't run out the bottom; make a little fold near the end to prevent this.

Tortillas are also good when you toast them on a very hot, lightly oiled griddle, turning them once. They become crispy, and you can break them into bite-size pieces to dip in salsa or bean dip.

Another way to use tortillas: place them on a hot griddle or skillet, put a slice of cheese on one half, then fold the other half over the cheese, making a little "sandwich." Turn it over and toast the other side. It's also good with a thin slice of onion and green pepper on top of the cheese before you fold it.

Mexican Huevos Revueltos

4 eggs
2 tablespoons water
1 tablespoon olive oil
1 small onion, chopped
1 small green pepper, chopped
1/4 teaspoon cumin seeds, crushed
1 teaspoon chili powder
3 tomatoes, peeled and chopped
(or small can of tomatoes)
1 stalk celery, finely diced
Tabasco sauce
salt and pepper

1. Heat olive oil in a large skillet. Add cumin seeds and chili powder, then add chopped vegetables, adding tomatoes after a few minutes. Sauté until the vegetables are almost soft. (If using canned tomatoes, drain them and add them now).

2. Season this sauce with a few drops of Tabasco, salt and pepper to taste.

3. In a bowl, beat the eggs with water, then pour eggs over the sautéed vegetables.

4. Cover pan and cook gently on low heat until eggs rise and are just set. Don't overcook as they will become "tough" and lose some of their flavor.

Served with Mexican beans and cornbread, this makes a very savory meal.

If you don't like the Mexican flavor, you can make a similar dish by pouring beaten eggs over sautéed bean sprouts, green onions and shredded snow peas. Cook only until the eggs begin to set. Try one of the sauces for stir-fry to spoon on the top.

Egg Replacer does well in these recipes.

Stuffed Green Peppers

4 whole green peppers with top and seeds removed
1 onion, chopped
4–6 cloves garlic, minced
1 cup walnuts
¹/4 cups butter or margarine
¹/2 cup bread crumbs
1 cup grated cheese
¹/4 cup sesame seeds
14 oz. can stewed tomatoes, seasoned
1 fresh tomato, chopped

1. Season stewed tomatoes (Karen uses onion, garlic, basil, and oregano, salt and pepper). Set aside in sauce pan that fits inside your pressure cooker.
2. Cook peppers in boiling salted water 5–10 minutes.
3. Melt butter in fry pan and cook onion and garlic until clear and tender, approximately 10 minutes. Add bread crumbs, chopped nuts and sesame seeds. Remove from heat and add grated cheese. Add seasonings as desired, i.e. curry powder, cayenne, black pepper, basil, nutmeg. Combine all ingredients well and stuff into pepper cavities.
4. Place stuffed peppers on stewed tomatoes in sauce pan inside the pressure cooker and top with chopped fresh tomato.
5. Put ¹/4 to ¹/2 cup salted water under the sauce pan in the pressure cooker. Bring to full pressure and then turn off heat. Allow to cool under pressure. Serve with rice.

This recipe is also from Karen on the Austrian sailing yacht "Flow." It was delicious the night she served it for dinner in the comfortable cockpit. Horst entertained us with his keyboard and the music filled the Hog Island anchorage.

Tamale Corn Casserole

1 egg, beaten
1 tablespoon butter or margarine
1/4 cup finely chopped onion
2 teaspoons chili powder
1/2 cup finely diced green pepper
1 can stewed tomatoes, strained
1 cup milk
3/4 cup coarse corn meal
1/2 teaspoon salt
1 scant tablespoon sugar
1 can corn
10 black olives

1. In a skillet, melt butter and sauté onion and green pepper. Add chili powder and cook briefly. Add strained stewed tomatoes.
2. In a medium-size sauce pan, bring milk to a boil. Slowly stir in salt, sugar, and corn meal, mixing until smooth.
3. Add corn, olives, and beaten egg, mixing well.
4. Stir the hot vegetables into the corn meal mixture.
5. Pour into a greased casserole and bake slowly until firm, about 30 minutes.

This recipe works very well cooked on top of the stove in a very heavy sauce pan. To prepare the pan, heat a very small amount of butter or margarine in the pan, coating all sides. Pour prepared corn mixture into the very hot pan, then cook slowly on very low heat to prevent burning the bottom while the mixture sets.

Kosheri with Fried Onion

1 can tomato sauce
salt and pepper
2 onions, sliced in rings for frying
2/3 cup low-fat milk or soy milk
1/2 cup all-purpose flour
1/4 cup corn oil
2 1/2 cups cooked long-grain brown rice
1 1/2 cups cooked green lentils
2 cups cooked whole-wheat macaroni

1. In a large sauce pan, heat tomato sauce over medium heat.
2. Soak onion rings in milk a few minutes, then drain. Put flour and onion rings in a paper bag and shake until onion rings are evenly coated. Place on paper towel for a few minutes.
3. Heat oil in a skillet, add onions and fry until crisp. Drain on paper towels and set aside.
4. To assemble kosheri, spoon rice onto a large serving platter. Pour 1/3 of the tomato sauce over the rice. Place lentils on top of rice, then spoon macaroni in center of lentils. Pour remaining tomato sauce over lentils and macaroni. Top with fried onions and a sprig of parsley. Alternatively, arrange on individual plates. Serve with Hot Sauce in a separate bowl.

Hot Sauce

1 teaspoon cumin
1 teaspoon coriander
1/2 teaspoon chili powder
1/2 teaspoon celery salt
4 tablespoons tomato purée
3/4 cup vegetable stock

Blend the spices and tomato purée. Add the vegetable stock and stir well to make a paste.

Soya Rissoles

1 cup soya granules (TVP mince)
1 cup hot water
1/2 teaspoon thyme
1/2 cup oats
1/4 cup whole-wheat flour
2 tablespoons yeast flakes
1 egg, or Egg Replacer
1/2 cup bread crumbs
2 tablespoons tamari
1/2 cup onions, finely chopped
1/2 cup green peppers, finely chopped
1 tablespoon sesame oil
1 tablespoon other oil (sunflower, corn, etc.)

1. Mix hot water and soya granules and let sit 10 minutes.
2. Sauté chopped onions and green peppers in oil mixture.
3. Mix all of the ingredients except oils and let sit 15 minutes.
4. Form rissoles using 2 large spoons or dampened hands, then fry until golden brown.

You can shape these any way you like: make hot-dog shape and place in buns; shape as burgers and put in hamburger buns; shape as little "logs," insert a small stick in the end, and serve as hors d'oeuvres; shape as little balls and serve with rice, noodles, or potatoes.

Tamale Pie

Filling
2 cups soya granules (mince-style TVP)
2 cups red chili sauce
$^1/_2$ cup green chilies, chopped
$^1/_2$ cup cheddar cheese, shredded
$^1/_2$ cup cream-style corn
$^1/_2$ cup black olives

Add soya mince to red chili sauce, stir, and simmer for 10 minutes. Combine green chilies, cheese, corn and olives.

Cornmeal Crust
$2^1/_2$ cups cold water
1 teaspoon salt
$^1/_2$ teaspoon chili powder
$1^1/_4$ cups yellow corn meal
$^1/_2$ cup cheese, shredded

1. Combine water, salt, chili powder and corn meal in sauce pan. Cook over medium heat until thick and stiff (about 10 minutes), stirring often.
2. Reserve $^3/4$ cup for topping. Line sides and bottom of a 1$^1/2$ quart (6 cup) casserole with the remaining mixture.
3. Fill with soya mixture, and top with heaping tablespoons of reserved corn meal mixture.
4. Sprinkle with shredded cheese. Garnish with black olives. Bake at 350°F for 30 minutes, or in Dutch oven on top of the stove for 30 to 45 minutes.

If you cook this in an "oven" on top of the stove, it improves if you let it sit for awhile before serving.

Spanish Tortilla

I would bet that you think a tortilla is a thin, flat corn meal or flour thing that you either roll up and eat like bread, or you put beans, salad, or whatever on, fold over and eat like a sandwich. Well, if you order tortilla in Spain, you are served a slice of an egg-and-potato "pie." It is delicious. It is served hot or cold as a snack or light meal anytime of day. You will find it in virtually every eating place you might go, therefore it is perfect for vegetarians who often have a hard time in Spanish restaurants, where almost every dish has meat in it. A meal of tortilla and salad, then perhaps a dessert, is something you can almost always find.

1/2 pound potatoes
2 eggs, beaten
1/2 onion, finely chopped
1/2 sweet red pepper
2 or 3 tablespoons olive oil
salt and pepper

1. Cut the potatoes into small pieces or slices.
2. Heat olive oil in a skillet, add the potatoes and fry until soft.
3. Add onions and red pepper and fry until everything is cooked, without allowing the potatoes to become crisp.
4. Drain, place the mixture in a dish, add the beaten eggs and mix well.
5. Put a little of the oil back in the skillet, heat, then add the potato and egg mixture. When cooked underneath, cover the frying pan with a plate and turn the tortilla onto the plate, then slide it back into the pan with the cooked side up. Cook the other side without allowing the tortilla to dry out.

Serve hot or cold with lettuce, avocado, and tomato salad.

Every area of Spain and each cook has his own version of this dish. However, they all are made of potatoes and eggs. Some don't like onions, some use green peppers, parsley, or garlic. Some cooks parboil the potatoes. This is my favorite method, because you don't use so much oil, and it produces a lighter dish. It keeps well, and is good to take on a picnic or outing. You can buy it already prepared in many bakeries and shops. It is a very popular Spanish dish.

The following is prepared like a regular meat loaf, but contains no meat. The flavors are fresh and it keeps well for sandwiches later.

Vegetable Loaf

2 tablespoons olive oil
2 medium onions, chopped
4^1/$_2$ oz. TVP mince (granules)
^{1}/$_2$ cup grated carrots
2 cups hot vegetable stock
1^1/$_2$ cups bread crumbs
^{1}/$_4$ cup oats
1 tablespoon mixed herbs (oregano, sage, rosemary, thyme)
3 tablespoons freshly chopped parsley
(or 1 tablespoon dried parsley)
2 cloves garlic, finely chopped
1 egg beaten, or 1 tablespoon soy flour
^{1}/$_2$ cup soy milk, or 1 cup yoghurt
1 cup water
2 tablespoons tamari
Sauce
1 can of tomatoes, chopped
1 can tomato paste
salt (optional) and freshly ground pepper to taste

1. In a large sauce pan, heat oil and sauté onions until lightly browned. Add the TVP and grated carrots, stir and cook for 2 minutes. Add the hot water or stock and simmer 4 minutes.

2. In a separate bowl, mix the bread crumbs, oats, herbs and garlic with 1 cup cold water. Stir in the egg (or soy flour) and leave to one side for 10 minutes.

3. Combine the cooked TVP with the bread crumb mixture, then add the milk (or yoghurt) and tamari. Mix well and season to taste.

4.   Place the mixture in a baking dish or loaf pan, patting into shape and leaving space around the sides for the tomato sauce to run.

5.   Combine chopped tomatoes, tomato paste and seasonings in a small saucepan, heat, then pour over the loaf.

6.   Bake in Dutch oven on top of the stove for about 1 hour.

Note: This dish is better if you can let it sit for an hour or so before slicing. Serve with a mushroom sauce as a variety. Or try it with a yoghurt and horseradish sauce.

I like to place small uncooked potatoes around the loaf before cooking. They will absorb some of the sauce while they cook, are delicious, and look pretty.

Leftovers make great cold sandwiches, with mustard or horseradish and lettuce.

This is a favorite meal on "Sandpiper." It is a good buffet dish and everybody likes it, even non-vegetarians, who often think I have prepared meat for them (and they wonder how I did it without a refrigerator!).

Vegetable

Side

Dishes

Dilled Carrots

carrots (as many as needed), thinly sliced
1 teaspoon green onion, thinly sliced
1/2 teaspoon dill
sherry (optional)

1. Put carrots and sliced green onions in a small pan. Boil or steam them in small amount of water (and optional sherry) until soft.
2. Stir in 1/2 teaspoon (or more) of dill and cover to steam for another minute, or until ready to serve.

Carrots keep well without refrigeration, therefore they are one of the vegetables I use almost daily. I prefer them uncooked, shredded or chopped in a salad or slaw, but I also use them cooked in soups and stews. As a side dish, they are tasty when lightly cooked with a little minced onion and seasoned with any of the following: parsley, dill, basil, mint, white pepper, nutmeg, cinnamon, or lemon juice. Cooked, mashed carrots make an excellent addition to gravy when stirred in as a thickening agent.

Savory Carrots

1 or 2 green onions, thinly sliced
1 stalk celery, sliced
1 teaspoon butter, margarine, or oil
4 medium carrots, sliced
1/4 cup water for steaming

1. Heat sauce pan and melt butter, margarine, or oil. Add green onions and celery and sauté for a minute.
2. Add sliced carrots, stir-fry for a minute, then add water and immediately cover with a tight-fitting lid. Steam for 5 minutes, shaking pan from time to time to mix veggies and water.
3. Remove lid, check that the carrots are cooked to your taste, then season with white pepper. Serve hot.

Eggplant Grenada

1 large eggplant
1 clove garlic
1 teaspoon (or more) butter
salt and pepper

1. Wash the eggplant. Make a slit in it and put the garlic clove inside the slit.
2. Bake in a moderate oven until the eggplant is soft.
3. Take it out of the oven and allow to cool for a few minutes. Cut open and scoop out the insides, placing the pulp in a bowl.
4. Mash, adding a little butter. Season with salt and pepper and serve hot.

Instead of baking, you can roast the eggplant by cooking it slowly in a skillet, turning it frequently to roast all sides. Or even better, cook it on the barbecue on a Sunday at Hog Island, Grenada, The West Indies.

Fried Eggplant Patties

1 lb. eggplant, peeled and diced
1 egg, beaten
2 tablespoons flour
salt and pepper
peanut oil

1. Boil the eggplant until tender.
2. Drain, then mash the eggplant and allow it to cool.
3. Mix the cooled eggplant, beaten egg, salt and pepper, and flour.
4. Fry in hot oil until brown. Drain on paper, and serve.

These patties are good served with rice. Also, they make a good sandwich. Try barbecue sauce on them.

Fried Eggplant

eggplant
whole-wheat flour
olive oil
paprika

1. Slice the unpeeled eggplant in $1/2$-inch slices and let the slices sit on paper towel for about 10 minutes. If the eggplant is very moist, sprinkle it with salt to draw out some of the water. Cover the top with paper towel too.
2. Flour both sides and let sit for a few minutes. Sprinkle the eggplant with paprika and then fry in plenty of hot olive oil. Drain on paper and serve.

When zucchini is available it is usually plentiful. My friends who grow vegetables are often overwhelmed by the amount of zucchini they harvest. They have many recipes using it. There is even a Ratatouille Pizza! I like them sliced and lightly steamed with a little crushed garlic, a sprinkle of oregano, and freshly ground pepper.

Sautéed Zucchini

4 medium zucchini
1/4 cup canned milk
1 egg
1 cup bread crumbs
flour, salt, pepper
2-3 tablespoons oil
grated Parmesan (optional)

1. Wash, then slice zucchini lengthwise; sprinkle with salt, pepper and flour.
2. Mix beaten egg and milk. Dip zucchini halves in this mixture, then roll in bread crumbs.
3. Heat oil in a skillet, then fry zucchini until golden. Be careful not to overcook. Sprinkle with Parmesan.

Spicy Potatoes

1 pound potatoes, quartered
1 onion
2 tablespoons butter, margarine, or oil
1 teaspoon chili powder
1/2 teaspoon curry powder
1/4 teaspoon nutmeg
1/4 teaspoon cinnamon

1. Boil potatoes until partially cooked, about 10 minutes.
2. Sauté the onion in the butter. When the onion is soft, add the spices and cook for a minute.
3. Add the potatoes, stir gently, and cook until the potatoes are done.

Maupiti Melange

When you must use canned vegetables, you can make them more interesting by using a variety of herbs and spices. They won't have the crispness of freshly cooked vegetables, but often they can taste almost as good. I sometimes mix several different vegetables together, season them, and add a sauce. At sea this can produce a quick, easy, yet satisfying meal. This is one of my "emergency" suggestions.

1. In a large sauce pan, sauté one sliced onion and one minced clove of garlic in butter.
2. Add one can of well drained small potatoes. Cook for several minutes.
3. Add a can of each of the following: peas, mushrooms, and corn, all well drained.
4. Simmer until everything is heated through. Season with a tablespoon of dry parsley, salt, and pepper. Vary the flavor by seasoning with various herbs such as oregano, thyme, marjoram, or spices like cayenne, nutmeg, or white pepper.

Tangy Yellow Pumpkin

3 tablespoons vegetable oil
1 teaspoon cumin seeds
1/4 teaspoon nigella seeds
2 onions, finely sliced
1-inch piece fresh ginger, peeled and finely sliced
1/2 teaspoon hot red chili powder (cayenne)
1/2 teaspoon turmeric
1 teaspoon salt
2 tomatoes, chopped
1 lb. yellow pumpkin, peeled, seeded and
cut into 1-inch pieces
2 tablespoons dried mango powder
1/2 teaspoon garam masala

1.   Heat oil in saucepan over high heat and add cumin and nigella seeds; they will pop and spatter at once. Add onion and ginger. Lower heat and stir-fry until mixture is a pale gold. Add chili powder, turmeric, salt, and tomatoes and stir-fry until tomatoes are soft.

2.   Add pumpkin pieces, stir well and cover. Reduce heat and cook until pumpkin is soft and tender.

3.   Add mango powder and garam masala; stir well and cook for a few minutes more.

The spices for this recipe can be found in specialty spice shops from Fiji to Gibraltar. I came across this recipe in a small Indian spice shop which I found tucked in a dim hallway behind a tailor shop and a locksmith in Gibraltar. If you do not have mango powder, try using a mashed fresh mango. For garam masala you can use regular curry powder with the addition of allspice, cinnamon, and nutmeg. This is a colorful and delectable vegetable to serve with plain rice.

Pumpkin and Banana

1 lb. pumpkin, roughly cut into 1-inch cubes
2 firm bananas
1-inch piece ginger, thinly sliced
2 teaspoons garam masala
2 teaspoons butter or oil

1. Steam pumpkin until it starts to soften
2. Melt butter in a skillet and sauté fresh ginger slices for a minute, then add garam masala.
3. Add cooked pumpkin.
4. Slice bananas into pumpkin and sauté for a few minutes.
5. Season with a little freshly ground pepper and nutmeg.

Garam masala is a spice mixture of black pepper, cumin seeds, cinnamon, cardamoms, cloves, and bay leaves. If you don't have it, you can add a dash of each to season the dish.

This is a good side dish served along with green beans, callaloo, or spinach, and perhaps cardamom rice to make a complete meal.

Green Beans with Ginger

1 pound green beans
1 onion, cut in half then thinly sliced
1 1/2-inch piece fresh ginger, thinly sliced
1 tablespoon oil
1 tablespoon tamari

1. Wash and trim the green beans. Either leave them whole, or slice diagonally or in short pieces.
2. In a skillet or sauce pan with a tight-fitting lid, heat the oil, then add the slices of onion and ginger. Cook over medium heat until onions become limp.
3. Add the green beans and ⅓ cup water, then cover the pan immediately to allow the beans to steam until done, adding more water if necessary.
4. Stir in the tamari. Serve hot.

Catalan Potatoes with "Oli-Oil"

Oli-Oil
Potatoes
parsley

1. Boil as many potatoes as you want for your meal.
2. Cut potatoes into quarters, place in a bowl and douse with Oli-Oil.
3. Chop a handful of parsley and sprinkle over potatoes.

Oli-Oil
2 cloves garlic
2-4 tablespoons olive oil

1. In a wooden mortar, or a wooden salad bowl, use a wooden pestle to crush the garlic. If you don't have a pestle, use a large wooden spoon.
2. While pounding the garlic, slowly add olive oil to make a paste. Continue pounding while adding the rest of the oil, mixing well. The mixture will become creamy. Season to your taste with salt and pepper.

Sweet-Sour Beets

1 can beets, or cooked fresh beets
1/2 cup vinegar
1/4 cup apple juice
2 tablespoons sugar
juice of 1/2 lemon
1/4 teaspoon cinnamon
4 cloves

1. If beets are large, slice or shred them. If they are baby beets, you can leave them whole.
2. Put all ingredients in a saucepan, cover, and simmer for 15 minutes. Serve hot or cold.

Breads,

Pancakes,

Biscuits

Southern Biscuits

2 cups flour, sifted (whole-wheat is best)
4 teaspoons double-acting baking powder
1/2 teaspoon salt
4 tablespoons margarine or oil
3/4 to 1 cup milk, buttermilk, or yoghurt

1. Sift together dry ingredients. Using two knives, cut in soft margarine; or, if using oil, stir it in with the milk or yoghurt, using enough milk to form a very soft dough. "Drop" by tablespoonfuls into a heavy skillet, cover with a lid, and cook over low heat for about 12 minutes, or until firm and brown on the bottom. Turn with spatula and allow the other side to brown.

2. Alternatively: use only about 3/4 cup milk or yoghurt to form dough. Roll out on floured surface to about 1-inch thickness, and cut into circles using a cookie cutter or a drinking glass of size desired (say about 2 inches). Place biscuits on a cookie sheet or in a pan and bake in preheated oven (400°F) for 12 to 15 minutes until brown on top. Serve hot with butter and jam, honey, syrup, or, as in the South, with gravy.

3. For variety, add any of the following: 1/4 cup finely chopped parsley; 1/4 teaspoon thyme, marjoram or basil; 3 tablespoons finely diced pimentos, celery, or grated onion; 2 teaspoons or more of poppy, sesame, or caraway seeds. The herb biscuits are really good!

I learned to sail in Corpus Christi, Texas. I was a member of the Mariner Scouts, and we had several types of sailboats for our use and care. One of the boats, the "Four Friends," was large enough for most of our members to be aboard at the same time, and what good times we had sailing around the bay and barrier islands. On a weekend cruise we anchored out for the night, but we always had a beach cookout in the evening. Often we were joined by the Sea Scouts, who had their own converted patrol boat (probably "scrounged" from the local Navy Base). The girls usually ended up being the cooks, and one of our more successful meals was "creamed-something" on biscuits. We cooked the biscuits in a heavy cast iron skillet with a cast iron lid, not unlike the wagon-train cook of a prairie schooner. I still use this method for cooking biscuits on my boat.

Duff

This is a quick and easy cobbler-like dish which was traditionally served for a special breakfast aboard the old sailing ships—possibly after successfully "rounding the Horn" or on Christmas Day. It is made on top of the stove, and the ingredients can be varied to use whatever you have available.

1 can of fruit with the juice—peaches, apricots, berries, apples
or
Fresh berries or fruit, cooked a few minutes with sugar to taste, to soften and form juice
¹/₂ recipe Southern Biscuits, adding some sugar to the dry ingredients and making dough a little softer than usual

1. Put the fruit and plenty of juice in a small sauce pan with a tight-fitting lid. Bring to simmer.
2. Drop the dough on top of the fruit mixture. Place the lid on the pot and simmer on very low heat for 12 to 15 minutes, until the dough is cooked. The liquid should bubble around the dough.
3. Serve hot in individual bowls "as is," or with milk, cream, or yoghurt. Of course, ice cream would be good too, but I've never been able to have it on my boat!

During the first few months after I became a "dropout" and moved on my boat, I cruised the Sacramento Delta in California. I was singlehanding and learning techniques and tricks that would later help me when I went further a-sea. Also, I was interested in provisioning a small boat for long periods of time, "just in case." Duff is one of the dishes I used to satisfy my sweet tooth. There were wild berries growing on the berms and levies around my boat, and the children on other yachts quickly learned that if they brought me a pot of these delicious fruits, I would treat them to some freshly-made duff. It is so quick and easy to make they could sit in the cockpit and watch the process while their mouths watered.

Pancakes

1¹/₂ cups whole-wheat flour
3 teaspoons double-acting baking powder
3 tablespoons oil
¹/₄ teaspoon salt (optional)
1 egg
1 cup sweet or sour milk, buttermilk, or yoghurt

1.   Sift the dry ingredients into a bowl. Add the milk, egg, and oil and stir just enough to mix well.
2.   Drop from tablespoon onto oiled, moderately hot griddle or frying pan; bake slowly until bubbles appear on the surface, then turn and brown on the other side
3.   Serve with honey, maple syrup, or jam.

Pancakes are always good for breakfast. They also make a good lunch or dinner main course. Try making very thin pancakes, or "crepes," and fill them with creamed vegetables. Roll them into a tube and put them on a plate with the ends tucked on the bottom. Top with a light cheese sauce or gravy, a few sprinkles of parsley, and you have a very attractive dish. Another method is to put the pancake on the plate, spoon the vegetable mixture on top of one half, then fold the other half over, making a folded pancake.

Using the same technique, but filling with fruit, you can make a fine dessert.

Another dessert can be made by placing one pancake on a plate, spoon fruit mixture on top, then put another on top of that, spoon more fruit and sauce on top, until you have as many layers as you want. Make a light custard or pudding sauce to drizzle over your creation. Yoghurt makes a good sauce as well.

Caribbean Rum Pancakes

2 cups flour
4 teaspoons baking powder
salt
1¹/₂ cups milk
2 tablespoons oil
1 egg
2 oz. rum
freshly grated nutmeg

1. Mix flour, baking powder, and salt.
2. Stir into the flour mixture the milk, egg, and oil, mixing gently.
3. Add the rum and stir until well-blended.
4. If possible, put in refrigerator to chill for about 15 minutes.
5. If batter has thickened, add a small amount more of milk, stirring very gently.
6. Heat a heavy skillet, using a very small amount of oil to coat the bottom. Cook the pancakes as you would regular pancakes. (I like to use only 1 tablespoon of batter for each little cake).
7. Serve with a dash of freshly grated nutmeg on the top.

In Mexico I learned to make tequila pancakes, so I decided to try rum while I was in the Caribbean. You can also flavor your honey or syrup with a very small amount of rum. This makes a nice change for breakfast or dessert.

Yeast Pancakes

1¹/2 cups whole-wheat flour
1-2 tablespoons yeast
2 teaspoons honey or sugar
¹/4 teaspoon salt (or as desired)
1¹/2 cups milk or yoghurt
1 egg, beaten
2 tablespoons oil

1. In a large bowl, mix the dry ingredients, then add the milk or yoghurt, egg, and oil. Stir well.

2. Bake immediately if 2 tablespoons of yeast are used; or better yet, let rise in a warm place 30 minutes or longer if 1 tablespoon is used. The batter will become very bubbly as it rises, so use a large bowl.

3. Bake on a moderately hot, lightly oiled griddle, using a tablespoon of batter for each pancake. Turn after only a few seconds when the bottom has browned.

These little pancakes are so delicious, and remind me of ones I had in a little Swedish pancake house in San Francisco. They look pretty placed in a circle on a preheated plate, one lapping over the other, forming a ring. You can put crushed fruit in the center. Any berry syrup is also good. If you want to get fancy, place a small amount of cream cheese on one half of the pancake, fold over the other half, and either put in a chafing dish, or directly on a warm plate, with each pancake overlapping the other. Pour berry syrup (raspberry or loganberry are good) along the center of the folded pancakes. This makes an attractive brunch dish. You can make the pancakes ahead of time and prepare the dish later, warming them well through before serving.

Whole-wheat Scones

3 tablespoons butter or margarine
2 cups whole-wheat flour
4 teaspoons baking powder
pinch salt
¹/₄ cup brown sugar
2 or 3 tablespoons chopped dates
1 egg, beaten,
¹/₂ cup milk

1. Mix flour, salt, and baking powder. Rub butter or margarine into the flour.
2. Add sugar, dates, and egg mixed with milk, reserving a little liquid for the glaze.
3. Mix well, then knead the mix lightly on a floured board.
4. Shape into a round and put on a greased tray or in a greased pan. Brush with remaining egg-milk mixture. With a blunt knife, lightly mark out 8 or 10 wedges.
5. Bake 15–20 minutes, either in oven or Dutch oven on top of the stove.

You can substitute cheese for dates, omitting sugar.
Soya milk in place of regular milk gives this bread a great flavor.

Kirsty brought this scrumptious coffee cake to me on Christmas Day in Secret Harbor, Grenada. I asked her for her recipe which she wrote out for me, adding the comment "A handy recipe for when you are too lazy to make bread, or the yeast has died on you!" Kirsty, from New Zealand, and Peter, from England are cruising in their Wharam Cat "Tekaroa."

Cinnamon Rolls

1 cup warm milk or water
3 cups whole-wheat pastry flour
(or mixture of white and whole-wheat)
salt
2 tablespoons butter or oil
1 beaten egg (or Egg Replacer)
1/4 cup honey or brown or raw sugar
1 tablespoon or 1 cake yeast
1/8 teaspoon vanilla
1/4 teaspoon nutmeg (optional)
butter or oil
brown sugar
cinnamon, nuts, raisins

1. Dissolve yeast in the warm liquid. Add salt, butter, honey or sugar, vanilla, and eggs.
2. Beat in half of the flour. Mix in flour until dough is easily worked but not sticky.
3. Let rise until double in bulk. Punch down and let rest while you butter or oil a baking pan.
4. Roll dough into a rectangle, then smear with butter or oil. Sprinkle with brown sugar, cinnamon, nuts, and raisins, as desired.
5. Roll into a tube, and slice into rounds about 1/2 to 3/4-inch thick, forming cinnamon swirls. Place in prepared pan. Bake in 365° oven for about 20 to 25 minutes.

Since I don't have an oven, I place the swirls in a very heavy skillet or pan and "bake" on top of the stove. Use a low heat so the bottom doesn't burn before they are cooked through. If you sprinkle a little cinnamon on the tops before cooking, you will have a brown top. Or, you can flip them over for a few minutes at the end of cooking, but this is not necessary. Serve hot. If there are any left over, they make delicious little cheese sandwiches.

Dainties

Several days before you want to make these little goodies, save some of the peel from an orange. Finely dice the peel, and put the pieces in a jar with 1 cup of sugar, mixing well.

1 cup warm milk or water
3 cups whole-wheat pastry flour
(or mixture of white and whole-wheat)
salt
2 tablespoons butter or oil
1 beaten egg (or Egg Replacer)
1/4 cup honey or brown or raw sugar
1 tablespoon or 1 cake of yeast
1/8 teaspoon vanilla

1. Dissolve yeast in liquid, then add salt, butter, honey, vanilla and egg.
2. Beat in half of the flour until dough is not sticky and is easily worked.
3. Let rise until dough has doubled in bulk. Punch down.
4. Roll dough into rectangle, smear with butter, margarine, or oil.
5. Sprinkle the orange-sugar mixture evenly over the dough.
6. Tightly roll the dough into a "log." Slice into 1/2-inch pieces and place in a greased pan.
7. Bake for 15–20 minutes at 375°F. Use very low heat if "baking" on top of the stove to prevent burning the bottom, or use a Dutch oven.

While we were passing the long hurricane season of 1976 in the isolated area of Conception Bay in Baja California, we did a lot of reading, snorkeling, and even (in some desperation) coloring! Our favorite books for coloring were cookbooks with line drawings which we transformed into colorful works of "art." Our provisions aboard "Sandpiper" were ample but simple, and we read with ardor any book that talked about food or drink. One book that we read was The Odyssey by Homer, in which the Greek sailors were always "mixing the wine" and preparing "dainties." I don't know what they meant by dainties, but I devised the above recipe as a modern-day substitute. Dainties became a frequent special treat. As for "mixing the wine," we had to settle for "T-'n-T," a mixture of tequila and grapefruit Tang.

Corn Bread

1 cup corn meal
1 cup flour
3 teaspoons double-acting baking powder
1 cup milk
1 egg
1/4 cup oil, margarine, or butter
1/4 teaspoon salt
1 tablespoon sugar (optional)

1. If using oven, preheat the oven to 400°F.
2. Put the oil or margarine in a very heavy skillet (preferably a cast iron one), and put it in the oven (or on a burner) to get very hot.
3. Mix the corn meal, flour and baking powder in a bowl. Lightly beat the egg, and add it with the milk to the flour mixture, stirring only enough to mix into the flour.
4. Stir the hot oil from the skillet into the batter, then immediately pour the batter into the hot skillet. Place in the oven and cook until done and brown on top (about 20 minutes).

Alternatively: Cook on top of the stove on low heat, covering the skillet with a lid. When the bread is done (firm to touch), you can slide it onto a plate, then gently flip it over into the hot skillet to brown the other side. Serve hot.

Options: try omitting the egg, and add one rounded tablespoon of soy flour, or use soy milk in place of milk. Also, you can use whole-wheat flour in place of white flour.

There are many variations on basic corn bread. Try adding: chopped and sautéed onions and green or red peppers; small chunks of cheese, herbs and spices like chili powder, cumin seeds, or paprika (either sweet or hot). We like corn bread split and served with basted eggs on top. Makes a good breakfast at sea.

Cheese 'n Chilies Cornbread

2 eggs, lightly beaten
1 cup plain yoghurt
1/4 cup melted butter, cooled
1 cup corn meal
1 teaspoon each salt and baking powder
1/2 teaspoon baking soda
1 cup grated Monterey Jack cheese
1 cup canned cream-style corn
1/2 cup minced green onions
1 (4 oz.) can chopped green chilies

1. Heat oven to 400°F.
2. Whisk together eggs, yoghurt and butter in a medium bowl.
3. Add dry ingredients and mix until just well blended.
4. Add remaining ingredients and mix well.
5. Pour into greased 10-inch heavy skillet and "bake" 40 minutes.

This dish makes a good, easy to prepare at-sea meal. You can use sour milk in place of yoghurt, or sweet milk without the soda. At sea, I have made it in my pressure cooker using low pressure and cooking for only 10–15 minutes with low heat.

I use my pressure cooker frequently, not only for foods that require long cooking, but also for casseroles that need baking. The top of the food doesn't get brown, but if you use the lowest amount of heat possible, the pot acts like a Dutch oven and most things come out very well.

You can use your pressure cooker to bake bread quite successfully. Make bread dough by the usual method, forming it into a round. Sprinkle a little corn meal in the bottom of the pot before you add the dough, and when it's cooked and you turn the bread upside-down, you will have a brown top. Leave the steam valve open to let the moisture escape while baking. The cooking time will be about the same as for an oven, about 45 minutes.

Corn Bread Pizza

¹/₂ cup corn meal
¹/₂ cup flour
¹/₂ tablespoon sugar
1 tablespoon yeast
¹/₄ teaspoon salt
2 tablespoons powdered milk
1 teaspoon mixed Italian herbs
¹/₂ cup warm water
1 egg
2 tablespoons butter or margarine
1 small onion sliced in rings
1 small green or red pepper sliced in rings
1 tomato peeled and thinly sliced (optional)
¹/₂ cup grated cheese

1. Mix the dry ingredients in a mixing bowl. Stir in the egg and the warm water, stirring just enough to moisten all the ingredients.

2. Melt the butter or margarine in a large skillet or frying pan. Lightly sauté the onion and pepper rings, then remove them to a saucer.

3. Pour the melted butter into the cornbread batter, stirring to mix. Let the batter sit for 15 minutes.

4. Spread the cornbread mixture over the bottom of the pan. Place the sautéed veggies on top of the cornbread, then the tomato slices (and whatever else you may want to add, including more herbs), and finally sprinkle the cheese on top of everything.

5. Put a tight-fitting lid on top of the skillet and cook on top of the stove very slowly for about 15 minutes, or until the bottom is brown and the top of the bread is done to the touch. Or, if you have an oven, cook at 400° for about 15 minutes.

Eat hot or cold.

(You can also just chop the onions and pepper and cheese and add it to the batter, then cook as you would cornbread).

Pizza

3 cups flour
1 teaspoon yeast
1 teaspoon sugar
1 cup warm water
2 teaspoons salt
¼ cup oil

1. Dissolve yeast and sugar in warm water. Let stand 10 minutes.
2. Mix in oil, salt and flour. Knead a few minutes. Let rise 1 hour.
3. Divide dough into two balls, roll out to desired thickness and, if cooking on top of the stove, put the flattened dough in a large skillet which has a good lid.
4. Spread tomato paste on top of the dough and add your favorite toppings and herbs, then sprinkle cheese over the top. Cover with lid.
5. Place the skillet on a very low flame, and bake until the cheese is melted and the veggies are soft. (Or you can bake it in an oven if you have one).

I like to sauté vegetables such as onions and green peppers a little before putting them on the tomato paste. Some other toppings are: mushrooms, olives, artichoke hearts, spinach, crushed garlic, green onion rings, and, of course, cheeses. Crumbled Roquefort cheese topping by itself makes a might tasty pizza. Favorite herbs include: oregano, basil, thyme, herbs de Provence, Italian herb mixture, and freshly ground black pepper.

This recipe came from the s/v "Fleetwood" and was given to me in Kieta, Papua New Guinea, in 1982. It made a welcome change in our menus and gives the "Sandpiper" and environs a savory aroma.

Zucchini Pancakes

1 pound small zucchini, grated
1 medium-size onion, grated
6 oz. feta cheese, crumbled
3/4 cup all-purpose flour
2 eggs
1/2 teaspoon salt (optional)
1 teaspoon dried dill
1/2 teaspoon black pepper
1/4 cup olive oil

1. Mix grated zucchini, onion, feta cheese, flour, eggs, and seasonings to make a thin batter.
2. Heat oil in a large frying pan over medium heat.
3. Drop batter by large tablespoonfuls into hot oil.
4. Flatten into pancakes and fry until golden brown, about 5 minutes on each side.
5. Drain on absorbent paper. Serve hot or cold.

Zucchini pancakes make a tasty dish to serve with brunch or dinner. Although feta cheese is the cheese of choice, I have made them with white cheddar, Monterey Jack, and even tofu. A tossed green salad goes well with them.

Sauces

and

Gravies

Garlic and Oil Sauce

12 cloves garlic
1/4 cup olive oil
1/4 cup chopped parsley
2 tablespoons chopped fresh oregano
(or 1/4 teaspoon crushed dried oregano)
3/4 teaspoon salt (optional)
1/4 teaspoon pepper

1. Remove excess papery skin from the garlic cloves, but do not peel the garlic. In a saucepan over low heat, add the garlic to the oil and cook slowly until the garlic is soft and lightly browned, about 20 minutes.
2. When the garlic is done, remove saucepan from heat; stir in parsley, oregano, salt, and pepper.
3. To serve, toss pasta and sauce. Let each person cut through skin of each garlic clove and spread some of the soft, sweet-tasting garlic on the pasta. This makes enough sauce to go with 1 pound of pasta, providing 4 servings.

Lemon Sauce

1 cup vegetable stock
2 tablespoons onion, finely minced
1/2 teaspoon salt
1/4 teaspoon freshly ground black pepper
4 tablespoons butter or margarine
2 egg yolks
4 tablespoons lemon juice
2/3 teaspoon grated lemon rind

1. Mix vegetable stock with onion, salt, and pepper and bring to a simmer.
2. Beat in butter or margarine and egg yolks and simmer until mixture thickens (about 2 to 3 minutes), being careful not to let boil.
3. Stir in lemon juice and grated rind.
4. Serve immediately over freshly cooked spinach, broccoli, or cauliflower.

Sauce for Stir-Fried Veggies I

1 tablespoon corn flour (corn starch)
1 teaspoon sugar (optional)
¹/₄ cup sake, sherry or white wine
1 cup water
1 tablespoon tamari

Mix the above ingredients in a small bowl or measuring cup. You can either cook the sauce in a small sauce pan, just until it becomes clear, or pour it uncooked over the partially cooked veggies, stirring often, until the sauce becomes clear and thickened. If you cook it separately, pour it over the veggies when they are served.

Sweet-Sour Sauce

¹/₃ cup tamari
¹/₃ cup vinegar
1 tablespoon cornstarch
1 cup water

1. In a small sauce pan, mix the ingredients and bring to a simmer, stirring continuously.
2. Cook only until mixture becomes clear, then remove from the heat.
3. Serve hot over crisp vegetables.

Variation: Cut very thinly on the diagonal a few slices of carrots, cucumber, and green onion. Add these to the above mixture while it is cooking. This makes a very good sauce to use over rissoles or "meatballs." For an appetizer, make tiny rissoles or "meatless-balls" fried very crisply. Put them in a bowl, pour the hot sweet-sour sauce over them, and serve them with toothpicks.

Sauce for Stir-Fried Veggies II

¹/₂ cup orange juice
¹/₂ cup apple juice
2 tablespoons sugar
2 tablespoons corn starch
3 tablespoons soy sauce
¹/₃ cup water

Follow the directions for the above sauces.

Tomato-Curry Sauce

1 tablespoon curry powder
¹/₂ teaspoon cayenne
3 tablespoons oil
2 cloves garlic, crushed
3 tablespoons flour
1 pound tomatoes, chopped
¹/₂ small pepper, chopped
1 cup vegetable stock or water
¹/₂ teaspoon basil
¹/₂ teaspoon oregano
1 tablespoon tamari

1.   In a skillet or sauce pan, heat the oil, add the curry powder and cayenne and cook for one minute, stirring continuously.
2.   Add the crushed garlic, then stir in the flour, mixing well.
3.   Slowly stir in the water to make a smooth mixture.
4.   Add the chopped tomatoes and peppers. Continue to stir until mixture thickens.
5.   Add the herbs and simmer gently for about 5 minutes.
6.   Stir in the tamari.
7.   Serve on vegetables, rice or noodles.

Miso Gravy

2 tablespoons flour
2 tablespoons oil
1 to 2 cups water or stock
miso (a piece about the size of a walnut)

1. In a skillet make a roux of 2 tablespoons of flour added to 2 tablespoons of hot oil. Let it cook until it just begins to brown, stirring constantly with a whisk.
2. Slowly add 1 to 2 cups water or stock, depending upon the thickness desired, again stirring constantly.
3. When thickened, take off the heat and add the miso which has been softened in a small amount of warm water. Mix well, and reheat the gravy, but do not let it boil.
4. Serve with potatoes, vegetables, lentil loaf, etc.

Also, you can sauté sliced onions in the oil before adding the flour. A clove or two of crushed garlic is good too.

Mushroom–Miso Sauce

Sauté some mushrooms in oil, butter, or margarine. Remove them from the pan. Make the above miso gravy as described, possibly a little thinner than for normal gravy. Add the mushrooms, then the miso.

Cucumber Yoghurt Sauce for Curries

1 or 2 cucumbers, quartered and chopped
1 cup yoghurt
1 clove garlic, crushed
1 teaspoon parsley
juice of 1/2 a lemon
1/4 teaspoon white pepper

Mix all of the ingredients and let stand in the refrigerator for several hours, if possible.

Tomato and Olive Sauce

2 1/2 pounds soft tomatoes
2 tablespoons olive or salad oil
1 medium-sized onion, finely chopped
1 clove garlic, minced
1 teaspoon sugar
3/4 teaspoon crushed red pepper
1 (8 oz.) jar green olives, drained, pitted ,and chopped
2 tablespoons grated Parmesan cheese
2 tablespoons chopped parsley

1. In a 5-quart saucepan over high heat, heat 3 quarts of water to boiling. Cut an "X" in the bottom of each tomato. Place half of the tomatoes in boiling water for 30 seconds. With a slotted spoon, remove tomatoes and allow to cool slightly. Repeat with remaining tomatoes. Peel tomatoes, then cut each in half. Remove stem end, then squeeze each tomato half to remove seeds. Coarsely chop tomatoes, discarding seeds.

2. In 12-inch skillet over medium high heat, in hot olive or salad oil, cook onion until tender. Stir in garlic; cook one minute. Add chopped tomatoes, sugar, and crushed red pepper; cover and simmer 15 minutes to blend flavors.

3. Remove skillet from heat; stir in olives, Parmesan cheese, and chopped parsley. Makes about 4 cups sauce, enough to serve over 1 pound of pasta, cooked, for 6 servings.

Cream Sauce or White Sauce

Adding a sauce, or gravy, to your meals will give variety and make your dishes more interesting. To make a good sauce is not difficult, but many new cooks tend to omit them from their meals. Sauces and gravies are basically the same thing, gravies being made from "drippings," while sauces are made with butter, margarine, or oil. They both use flour and a liquid, both of which may be varied to produce different flavors. From the basic "white sauce" or "cream sauce," you can make cheese sauces, onion sauce, herb sauce, garlic sauce, miso sauce, etc. None of them take but a few minutes to prepare, and they add so much to the meal.

The most important thing is to keep the sauce or gravy light and clean-tasting. While the proportions are fairly standard, there might be a slight variation depending on the type of flour used, but not much.

To destroy any raw flour taste, simmer the sauce for at least 10 minutes, stirring with a wire whisk to produce a smooth texture.

Use whole-wheat flour for a nutty flavor and a rich color. For a creamier sauce, use a little extra powdered milk if you are using dry milk.

Consistency	Milk (or liquid)	Flour	Butter (or margarine)
Thin	1 cup	1 tablespoon	1 tablespoon
Medium	1 cup	2 tablespoons	2 tablespoons
Thick	1 cup	3 tablespoons	3 tablespoons

1. In a sauce pan or skillet, over low heat, melt the butter or margarine.
2. With a wire whisk or fork, blend in the flour. Do not brown.
3. Immediately after blending in the flour, slowly add the milk, stirring constantly with wire whisk. Add a bit more milk if sauce gets too thick. Allow to simmer very slowly for about 10 minutes, stirring constantly.

Variations:

Add any of the following during the last five minutes of cooking: mushrooms, celery, chives, finely minced onions, garlic, chopped boiled eggs, chopped ripe or green olives.

Vary seasonings with black or white pepper, curry powder or herbs.

Yoghurt Sauce

1 cup yoghurt
2 tablespoons lemon juice
1/2 teaspoon lemon rind, finely grated
1 teaspoon tamari
1/2 teaspoon dry mustard
4 tablespoons finely chopped green onion
cayenne pepper

1. Mix all of the ingredients. Serve with raw or chilled steamed vegetables.

You can make other yoghurt sauces by adding any of the following ingredients to one cup of plain yoghurt: crushed clove of garlic; 1 to 3 teaspoons curry powder; well-drained pineapple, with several teaspoons curry powder; dill weed; chili powder to taste; and horseradish.

Brown Gravy

2–4 tablespoons butter or margarine
4 tablespoons whole-wheat flour
1/2 teaspoon salt
2 cups vegetable stock or water
1/4 teaspoon freshly ground black pepper
1 tablespoon yeast extract
(or yeast flakes)

1. In a skillet or sauce pan melt the butter or margarine. Mix in the flour and salt using a fork or a wire whisk. Allow to cook over low heat for a few minutes until the flour turns light brown.
2. Slowly add the liquid, stirring continuously as the mixture thickens.
3. Stir in the yeast extract or yeast flakes and pepper.
4. Serve hot over lentil loaf, potatoes, vegetable loaf, rissoles, or rice.

Desserts

and

Sweets

Bananas and Rhubarb

2 cups diced rhubarb
1/2 cup sugar
2 bananas
1 cup yoghurt
1 cup vanilla wafers, crumbled
(or granola)

1. Combine rhubarb and sugar in a small amount of water and cook until the rhubarb is soft.
2. Slice the bananas into the bottom of dessert bowls, and add warm rhubarb sauce. Allow to cool.
3. Add crumbled cookies (or granola), then spoon yoghurt over all.

Variation: Make a thin custard sauce with corn flour (corn starch), milk, sugar, and vanilla, and pour over bananas and rhubarb. Then add crumbled wafers on top.

Or, put the vanilla wafers on the bottom, add bananas and rhubarb, then pour the custard over all, adding crumbled wafers on top.

A sprinkle of freshly grated nutmeg on top is good, too.

Bananas in Rum Sauce

4 bananas, peeled and sliced lengthwise
2 tablespoons butter
1/4 cup rum
2 tablespoons brown sugar
1 lime

1. In a large skillet melt butter.
2. Sauté the bananas in the butter until lightly browned.
3. Sprinkle sugar, then rum over the bananas. Cover and continue to cook for 2 or 3 minutes.
4. Add a few drops of lime juice on top. Serve plain, or with cream.

Pie Crust

1 heaping cup whole-wheat pastry flour
(or unbleached white flour)
pinch of salt (optional)
1/4 cup safflower oil, chilled
1 egg white, lightly beaten
(or Egg Replacer)
1 teaspoon apple cider vinegar
cool water as needed

1. In a medium bowl, mix flour and salt. Make a well in the center of the flour and add oil. Lightly mix with a fork or your fingers until you have a cornmeal-like texture.

2. Add egg white and vinegar to dough. Mix lightly with a fork or fingertips. Gently form dough into ball. Add water, a tablespoon at a time if necessary, making a sticky dough that holds together. Wrap in plastic or waxed paper. Chill 20 minutes or more.

3. Roll out the dough to 11 inches on a lightly floured surface. Place dough in a 9-inch pan (don't stretch it). Trim excess, leaving 1/2 inch overhang. Flute the edges for an elegant crust.

It is best if you can chill the unbaked shell. Bake it in a Dutch oven (or an oven, if you have one) for 8 to 10 minutes, then allow to cool. Fill with your favorite filling, or use it unbaked for pumpkin pie. (See recipe for Tofu Pumpkin Pie).

This is the way my grandmother made a pie crust, and her pies were always delicious. It makes a light and flaky crust which is very good with pies like pumpkin, apple sauce, and banana cream. I remember when she had an ice box instead of a refrigerator, similar to the galley aboard "Sandpiper" (although I seldom buy ice). She didn't have a thermostat in her oven either, but her breads and pies were always perfect.

Tofu Pumpkin Pie

20 oz. firm tofu
2/3 cup honey
2 egg whites, or equivalent amount of Egg Replacer
1³/4 cup fresh, cooked (or canned) pumpkin
2 teaspoons ground cinnamon
1 teaspoon ground nutmeg
1/2 teaspoon ground allspice
1/2 teaspoon ground ginger
1/4 teaspoon salt (optional)
1 unbaked deep-dish pie crust

1. Mash tofu with a fork or wire whisk until creamy and smooth.
2. Mix Egg Replacer with water as directed on package, or beat egg whites until frothy.
3. Add honey, egg whites, pumpkin, and spices; blend well.
4. Pour into an unbaked 9-inch deep-dish pie shell.
5. Bake in a Dutch oven (or a regular oven at 400°) for about 1 hour, or until a toothpick inserted into the center of the pie comes out almost clean.
6. Cool and serve.

Pumpkin is a staple food in the Caribbean, unlike in the States where it is seen mostly at Halloween. It makes a good, colorful, and nutritious addition to the table as a vegetable side dish, and it is used in soups and desserts as well. Fresh tofu can be hard to find in the supermarkets, but you can find it in UHT boxes in many natural food stores.

Lemon Cheese Pie

Graham Cracker Crust

*1¹/₂ cups smashed graham crackers
(or any bland cookies)
2 tablespoons sugar (optional)
¹/₃ cup melted butter*

1. In a bowl, mix all of the ingredients.
2. Place the mixture in a pie pan and pat to form an even pie shell.
3. You can bake with moderate heat for 8–10 minutes, then cool, or use unbaked.

(To easily mash the graham crackers without getting crumbs all over the sole, put them in a plastic bag and knead it with your hands. Or, put them in a wooden bowl and crush them with a big wooden spoon).

Lemon-Cheese Filling

*1 can sweetened condensed milk
¹/₂ cup lemon or lime juice
1 large package cream cheese*

1. In a medium-size bowl, mash softened cream cheese with a fork to a smooth paste.
2. Stir in condensed milk, mixing until smooth.
3. Thoroughly mix in the lime or lemon juice to form a smooth, thick mixture.
3. Pour into cooled graham cracker crust. Let stand to set.

This is a very easy cheesecake-type dessert. You can put your favorite fruit on top, making a pretty dish.

I think banana pudding with vanilla wafers has always been my favorite dessert. I remember preparing it for a "come over for coffee and dessert" evening when we were anchored in Port Sandwich in the New Hebrides. Our guest was the captain from a small coaster that anchored next to us. He was Polish, and although he didn't speak much English, we had good conversation, mostly about his sea career and isolated anchorages. He was delighted to be invited, and since we were a long way from any kind of shopping, I had to make-do. This banana pudding is what I served, and he devoured it. I can't make it quite like my mother did, because it requires a hot oven to toast the meringue; however, this is my version which seems mighty tasty in a quiet tropical anchorage.

Old-Fashioned Banana Pudding with Vanilla Wafers

4 tablespoons cornstarch
1/4 teaspoon salt
2/3 cup sugar
2 cups milk
1 teaspoon vanilla
1 tablespoon butter
vanilla wafers
bananas

1. In a sauce pan, mix cornstarch, salt, sugar and milk.
2. Bring to a boil over low heat and cook until thickened, stirring continuously.
3. Take off heat, allow to cool slightly, then stir in vanilla and butter.
4. Line a loaf pan, or your favorite serving bowl, with a layer of vanilla wafers.
5. Add a layer of sliced bananas.
6. Pour in some cooled pudding.
7. Repeat until all of the pudding has been used, ending with vanilla wafers placed on top.
8. Chill, if possible, or just let sit in a cool place for awhile before serving so the flavors can blend.

You really should have an oven or broiler (griller) to make this pie, but I am including it because it is so popular, especially in the Caribbean where limes are so plentiful and flavorful—I think they have a special taste here. You need the oven only for browning the top, but, if you make one to share with someone in your anchorage who has an oven, they will probably be more than happy to do it for you.

Key Lime Pie

4 eggs, separated
16 oz. condensed milk
5 oz. fresh lime (or lemon) juice
4 oz. sugar
1 large pie shell, pre-baked
(or graham cracker, etc.)

1. Beat egg yolks until light, then gradually beat in condensed milk and juice. Continue beating for another 2 minutes.
2. Put the lime filling into the pie shell.
3. Beat egg whites with sugar until very stiff.
4. Pile the beaten egg whites on top of the lime filling, making sure it joins the crust.
5. Place under hot grill until lightly browned, then chill.

Coconut Pie Crust

1¹/2 cups coconut, freshly grated or toasted shreds
¹/3 cup oil or butter
1 teaspoon finely grated lime or lemon rind

1. Mix all of the ingredients and press into a pie pan.

This is such a simple pie crust to make, and doesn't need baking. I like to fill it with vanilla, coconut, or banana pudding. Equally good is a mixture of fruits mixed with yoghurt or pudding. I learned to make this in Hawaii, where my friend made little individual pies in a muffin tin containing fluted paper liners into which she pressed the coconut pie crust mixture. She drizzled melted chocolate in each one, then filled them with mango pudding.

Quick Peanut Butter Sweets

¹/2 cup natural-style peanut butter
¹/2 cup honey
1 cup powdered milk

Blend the honey and peanut butter, then stir in the powdered milk. Spread on a buttered plate to about ³/4-inch thick. Cut into small cubes. Let sit for awhile, if you can.

Or, make into a roll, coating the outside with broken or chopped nuts or coconut, then slice. You can also form little balls with the mixture.

This is a very easy candy to make and is sure to satisfy your sweet tooth. It's an old recipe from my mother, and I remember her making this when I was a child. The kids in the anchorage will like it as a special treat, and the ingredients are usually found on any cruising boat.

Appendix

Measurements and Conversions

STANDARD MEASUREMENTS

1 teaspoon	=	1/6 fluid ounce
1 tablespoon	=	1/2 fluid ounce
1 cup	=	8 fluid ounces

EQUIVALENTS

1 tablespoon	=	3 teaspoons
1 cup	=	16 tablespoons
1/4 cup	=	4 tablespoons
1/2 cup	=	8 tablespoons

METRIC CONVERSIONS

Liquids

1 fl oz	=	25 ml
3 fl oz	=	75 ml
4 fl oz	=	100 ml
5 fl oz	=	125 ml
6 fl oz	=	150 ml
7 fl oz	=	175 ml
8 fl oz	=	200 ml
9 fl oz	=	225 ml

Solids

1 oz	=	25 g
2 oz	=	50 g
3 oz	=	75g
5 oz	=	150 g
6 oz	=	175 g
7 oz	=	200 g
8 oz (1/2 lb)	=	225 g
9 oz	=	250 g

TRANSLATIONS

1 English pint	=	20 fl oz
1 American pint	=	16 fl oz
1 English quart	=	32 fl oz
4 oz butter	=	1 stick butter
cornflour	=	cornstarch
tin	=	can

1 lb fat	=	2 cups
1 lb flour	=	4 cups
1 lb sugar	=	2 cups
1 lb br. sugar	=	**2-1/2 cups**
1 lb rice	=	2 cups
1 lb lentils	=	2 cups

New or Unfamiliar Words

Ghee

Ghee is clarified butter. It can be heated to high temperature without burning, so it is superb for frying. It keeps well without refrigeration.

To make ghee, take ordinary butter and simmer over low heat for 1½ hours. Strain into a container with a tight fitting lid.

Tamari

Tamari is a fermented product made from water, soy beans, wheat and salt. It is usually aged at least 18 months, making a dark brown clear liquid which both flavors and salts food. It is similar to soy sauce, but is far superior in flavor. Two tablespoons of Tamari is equivalent to about 1½ teaspoons salt.

Tahini

Tahini is made of crushed and hulled sesame seeds. It is used in sauces and gravies, salad dressings, spreads, deserts, and candies. It looks like peanut butter, but it is a little thinner. If it becomes too thick, soften it in a little warm water before adding to dishes. Tahini can be used like peanut butter for sandwiches, and a tablespoon added to your burger-patty mix will add an pleasing piquancy. Try a Tahini sauce to put over fried or grilled eggplant. Tahini is an excellent source of protein and very delicious. Up to now, I have found it only in specialty shops and particular super markets.

TVP

Textured Vegetable Protein is a dry product made from the soy bean. Over the years I have seen much improvement in TVP, and now you find many forms of it, including mince, granules, and chunks which are great for stews. The flavor has improved as well as the texture. It is an excellent source of protein and is excellent for cruising boats without refrigeration for it keeps like rice or pulses. It can be flavored as you like, or you can buy it already flavored. It is so handy to use, for example, add a handful to your spaghetti sauce while it simmers. It isn't always necessary to soak it (in fact, often I find it preferable not to presoak it). It can be sautéed along with the onions and garlic, absorbing their flavors, then you add the liquid as you normally do in your recipe. TVP mince is perfect for making tacos, tamale pie, sloppy joes and pizza; the granules are excellent in a Vegetable Loaf, or "meatless loaf," rissoles, and burger patties. It takes a little practice to get the burger patties to hold together, but with a little experimentation and ingenuity you'll make savory dishes that anyone would like.

Some Substitutions

Honey	for	Sugar
Eggplant	for	Mushrooms
Vinegar	for	Lemon Juice
Yoghurt	for	Sour Cream
Tofu	for	Cheese
Carob	for	Chocolate
Whole wheat flour	for	white flour
Soy Milk	for	milk
Soy Butter	for	Butter
Tamari	for	Salt

Some Favorite Menus Aboard the *Sandpiper*

Curried Vegetables On Rice, Lentils
Cucumber Yoghurt Sauce
⚓

Spaghetti With Tomato-Basil Sauce
Green Salad
⚓

Mexican Beans, Rice
Corn Bread
⚓

Buckwheat Noodles With Champignon Sauce
Tossed Green Salad
⚓

Vegetable Stew
Hot Garlic French Bread
⚓

Mexican Rice, Corn, and Cole Slaw
⚓

High Water Gibraltar
Sweet Sour Beets
⚓

Tamale Pie
Fruit Cole Slaw
⚓

Spinach Cannelloni
Carrot Salad
⚓

Vegetable Loaf with Potatoes
Green Beans
⚓

Catalan Alubias with Aselgas
Fried Eggplant
⚓

Stir–Fried Veggies, Rice
Rissoles, Tamari Sauce
⚓

Penne Regate With Green Pepper Sauce
Tomato Salad
⚓

Cous Cous With Curried Veggies, Yoghurt
⚓

Lentil Loaf with Cardamom Rice and Carrots
⚓

Altea Attraction
Green Salad
⚓

Spinach Noodles with Sautéed Mushrooms
Dilled Carrots
⚓

Cauliflower and Fennel Pie
⚓

Fried Rice, Peas, Carrot Salad
⚓

Hot and Spicy Mexican Rice
Mixed Fruit Salad
⚓

Marinated Garbanzos, Cole Slaw
Macaroni-Olive Salad
⚓

Potato Salad, Fruit Cole Slaw, Nice and Spicy Rice
⚓

INDEX

Index

Other Books Available From

Seaworthy Publications

Lightning and Boats, A Manual of Safety and Prevention
by Michael V. Huck, Jr.

Since man first plied the oceans, the threat of lightning strikes while on the water has ranked as one of the most feared and least understood of natural phenomena to confront the seafaring voyager. Lightning is like many of nature's more flamboyant manifestations; it is surrounded by legend, old wives' tales, and some outright errors. The unpredictable nature of the event has contributed to the sometimes contradictory advice on how to prevent lightning from striking, and how best to minimize injury or damage should a strike occur.

Lightning and Boats examines the phenomenon of lightning and provides the boater a **three-tiered approach** to safety and strike prevention. Starting with avoidance, the book describes low-cost equipment that any boater can employ to reduce the likelihood of a strike occurring. Next discussed is the subject of proper grounding and safety precautions to protect the crew and vessel should the worst case scenario of an actual strike occur. Finally, the secondary effects of lightning are discussed with regard to controlling the potential for adverse effects on installed equipment; this last tier being the most common result of a strike or near strike, especially among unmanned boats at moorings or while out of the water.

Lightning and Boats **provides boaters with the facts and theories necessary to make intelligent determinations about their own boats' lightning safety and enables them to prescribe safety modifications if necessary. The book is a 1995 release consisting of 80 pages of information, spectacular photos of lightning strikes, diagrams, glossary and reference material list. The price is only $9.95.**
ISBN 0-9639566-0-4

*"Anyone who plans to use one of my static dissipators on their boat should get a copy of this book"...**Bruce Kaiser, President of Lightning Master Corp.***

*"...does a good job of explaining to the layman the lightning phenomenon and how to protect boats from it."...**Practical Sailor.***

*"...examines lightning itself, using specific explanations to dispell the myths surrounding it...explaining how to deal with lightning at sea, focusing on equipment, technique, and effect...proper grounding and safety precautions and the damage that can result from a lightning strike on a boat's electrical system and structural integrit."...**Soundings.***

*"...everything from the propagation of lightning to seamanship during an actual storm...features the latest findings from NASA and companies protecting the transmission facilities of the cellular telephone networks and applies them to the electronic-rich environment of today's vessels"...**Southern Boating Magazine.***

*"...worth reading for a more detailed understanding of lightning and protective measures...focuses tightly on the phenomenon, and champions static dissipation as a method to help reduce the likelihood of a strike"...**Lakeland Boating Magazine.***

*"...eexamines the lightning phenomenon and provides boaters with a three-tiered approach to safety and strike prevention"...**Power and Motor Yacht.***

*"...A fascinating little book packed with information...Huck tackles the subject with brevity and insite...It is rare that I read a book that inspires me to dash out to my boat and start working, but that was the case with Lightning and Boats."...**Sailing Magazine***

Other Books Available From

Seaworthy Publications

The Exuma Guide, A Cruising Guide to the Exuma Cays
by Stephen J. Pavlidis

A completely up-to date, thoroughly researched, painstakingly detailed cruising guide to the Exuma Cays, *The Exuma Guide,* by Stephen J. Pavlidis is the most current, comprehensive, and all-encompassing cruising guide ever written about the Exuma Cays. The volume is loaded with detailed information, fabulous sketch-charts, photographs, and local knowledge of the Exuma Cays. Steve Pavlidis, while serving as a Deputy Warden of the Exuma Cays Land and Sea Park, wrote this guide over three years of extensive research in and around the Exuma Cays. Nothing has been overlooked as Steve guides you in and out of virtually every navigable harbor, cove, pass and anchorage, as well as around every major reef, head, sand bank and obstacle, throughout the entire Exumas island chain.

Much of what Steve has written in *The Exuma Guide* is not available from any other publication. Local knowledge is the key, and in *The Exuma Guide* you get information previously known only to those who live there. The book will supplement your charts and other "official" information with the specifics of how things really are and what to watch out for and avoid. The masterfully drawn sketch-charts will point out many details and variances that are overlooked or incorrect in the standard regional charts.

The Exuma Guide contains lists of information on GPS waypoints, marine facilities, customs regulations, beacons and navigational aids, distances, ham and weather radio broadcasts and stations, anchoring tips, tides and currents, as well as phone numbers, reference reading, and even local recipes, holidays and customs.

The books consists of 226 pages, with 60 sketch-charts, a sketch-chart index, aerial photographs, full-color cover, table of contents, text index, and bibliography. The price is only $24.95. ISBN 0-9639566-1-2

"Using a small skiff, Pavlidis investigated the islands, coves, cuts and harbors of the Exumas, taking, he writes, 'thousands of soundings up and down the entire island chain, from Sail Rocks in the north to Sandy Cay in the south, and in and out of all the cuts and passes between them. I have trod each and every shoreline and poked the bow of my dinghy into every nook and cranny in these cays, regardless of how isolated they may be.' The result of this patient research is 60 sketch charts....carefully drawn and amazingly detailed....include routes for both deep....and shallow draft vessels....sailing directions are easy to follow...for the uninitiated, navigating the [Exumas] could be a bit daunting. 'The Exuma Guide' pretty much takes care of that."....Bill Schanen, Sailing Magazine

Seaworthy Publications

Writer's Guidelines

Seaworthy Publications is a small press in southern Wisconsin dedicated to publishing books about sailing and boating. We actively solicit the unpublished works of authors interested in writing for us.

You can obtain a copy of our Writer's Guidelines by sending a self-addressed, stamped envelope to:

Seaworthy Publications
17125C W. Bluemound Rd.
Suite 200
Brookfield, WI, 53008-0949